RADIOPHONIC TIMES

40 Years with the Radiophonic Workshop, in the studio and on the road

PETER HOWELL

RADIOPHONIC TIMES

ISBN: 9781913456061

Published by Obverse Books, Edinburgh

Cover Design: Cody Schell

First edition: March 2021

10 9 8 7 6 5 4 3 2 1

Text © 2021 Peter Howell

Quotation from *A Brief History of Time* (1988) by Professor Stephen Hawking on page 171 used by permission of his Estate.

No part of this publication may be reproduced, stored in a retrieval system, or transmitted, in any form or by any means without the prior written permission of the publisher, nor be otherwise circulated in any form of binding or cover other than that in which it is published and without a similar condition being imposed on the subsequent purchaser.

A CIP catalogue record for this title is available from the British Library.

RADIOPHONIC TIMES

40 Years with the Radiophonic Workshop, in the studio and on the road

RADIOPHONIC TIMES

I have spent my whole career convinced that
one day I would be found out…
this is the day

RADIOPHONIC TIMES

Before We Start

This is a book about the past and the present. How in 1974 I found myself at the BBC Radiophonic Workshop, and following its closure in 1998, how five of us formed a band.

I use present day concerts as springboards, bringing events from the past to mind. So, I make no apology for darting around in time. I don't imagine Doctor Who would find the need to apologise for that either, so I'm in good company.

I hope I can give an impression of what it was like to work at the Radiophonic Workshop, the odd techniques we developed to tease out new sounds from brute machines, and how technology gradually evolved from the downright impossible to the 'do it all' era of the computers.

There could be as many books as there were composers at the Workshop. I can only tell my own story and will not pretend to tell theirs. Where appropriate, they come into the narrative, but this is not an exercise in name dropping, nor is it a catalogue of quotes. It's the story of someone who was in the Radiophonic Workshop for twenty-six years, and whose career would have been nothing without it.

I've gained a rather dubious reputation over the years for unusual analogies, so those of you who like your metaphors mixed are in for a treat, but one thing I won't be doing is describing the waveform page of the Fairlight Computer Instrument as a cake! I did that in front of a group of schoolchildren who were visiting the Workshop in the eighties, only to realise half way through that for the metaphor to work, the cake would have to be sliced horizontally. The head of the Workshop, Brian Hodgson, made me promise never to do it again!

The book is divided into three parts. These correspond to the three ages of the Radiophonic Workshop.

When I first went to the workshop in 1974, its pioneering early period was drawing to an end. John Baker was still hard at work, but elsewhere there were already signs of what was to come. Early synthesisers were already challenging the old ways, but the list of programmes still featured many classically inventive scores, such as *Dial M for Murder* and Paddy Kingsland's **The Changes.**

From around 1978, armed with an ever-increasing amount of new equipment, we embraced what would become the middle period. Technologically inventive and exciting, but a rather eclectic mix of gear in need of careful handling. An era that saw our involvement with **Doctor Who** blossom, and our popularity inside the BBC reach its peak. This was a period that saw an increasing number of scores for major series, such as **The Living Planet**, scored by Elizabeth Parker, and Roger Limb's for **The Box of Delights**. We were producing music and sound that still stood out for its originality.

From 1985, when we took delivery of our first computers, we were swept along on an unstoppable wave of digital technology. A new and challenging change of style that would characterise our third and final period. As well equipped as any outside composer, we could now produce conventional scores as well as the more experimental material that had been our stock in trade.

The proliferation of digital technology would eventually lead to our decline, and our exit from the BBC after forty years of work.

But we'll not stop there. This is not an exercise in looking back. The Workshop still exists as a band. With an act based on all the previous BBC material, together with new music made with today's array of electronic instruments and software, we give people a chance to experience live what they had previously only imagined. The Workshop full of strange gear being poured over by a band of maverick musicians.

The Radiophonic band has given me the opportunity to write lyrics and compose music, which is a welcome return to the old days[1] for me. Throughout my time at the workshop, that had been impossible.

So, writing this book has brought all those strands together and reminded me just how much we all packed into those 40 years.

Inevitably, in trying to remember what happened and when, I've used various sources for research.

One of the most useful of these is the excellent site that our long time engineer, Ray White, has put together at https://whitefiles.org/rwi/

This serves as a reliable engineering history of the Workshop and has been invaluable in confirming what I remember, and even reminding me of things I'd completely forgotten.

Firstly though, we need to delve into the more recent past.

---

[1] Before I joined The BBC.

RADIOPHONIC TIMES

Part 1

Now and Then

Festival No 6

A Toe in the Water

We are playing at the Festival No 6 in Portmeirion tonight.

It's September, 2013. Paddy Kingsland, Roger Limb, Dick Mills, Mark Ayres and myself are in North Wales.

To be exact, we are suspended hundreds of feet above a Welsh valley in a transit van, travelling uncomfortably fast towards Portmeirion. This is a long split Transit, with seating in the middle, and all the gear squeezed into the rear section. Our driver and tour manager, Ollie Cater, is convinced that the Sat Nav never lies and, ignoring our subtle hints about 'A' roads and motorways, sticks to the scenic route all the way. The Radiophonic Workshop has never played at a festival and it might go horribly wrong.

In 2009, we got together at the Roundhouse[1] for a one off evening of Radiophonic nostalgia and haven't played live since. In any case, this is different. There are going to be three stages at this festival, and plenty

---
[1] More later about this gig.

of choices. If the concert goers don't fancy it, they won't come, and we'll simply have to pack our stuff back in the van and head home (hopefully on the motorways).

The scene in the van is as you might expect. Paddy, Roger and Dick are in the back seat, talking non-stop. Life at the Workshop in the seventies, the sometimes bizarre antics of our founding leader Desmond Briscoe, the wayward nature of most of the gear, all being thoroughly picked over. Mark is beside me, head bowed over a laptop, creating the video that will accompany one of our numbers. I'm unemployed. Idly staring at the passing scenery, which seems a long way away, and a very long way down. This is a typical snapshot of the five of us. I have always operated at full tilt but in waves, the peaks are intense but the troughs catatonic. Mark is in a constant stream of activity, and Paddy and Roger are enthusiastic and willing to contribute whenever necessary. Dick, being the elder statesman of the bunch, is always supportive and as genuinely funny as ever.

We are arriving at Portmeirion now. I've been here before, but not like this. To me, this is the mecca for fans of **The Prisoner**[2], but now it's invaded by music lovers, marquees and stalls. The van's directed to an area behind the stage in a large marquee. Kieron Pepper, our drummer and invaluable source of confidence at any gig[3], has arrived independently and unloaded his kit. It's now raining heavily, and as we move our gear through the back entrance, a large canvas flap pours rainwater on our heads.

I'm ignorant of backstage protocols at an event like this. The greatest challenge is dealing quickly with a succession of bands, and their associated equipment. Being known for our vintage gear and unusual sound, travelling light's not an option for us, so we suffer more than most at festivals. We manhandle the gear on to three mobile rostra. These so-called 'trucks' are wheeled into position on stage when our time's due,

---

[2] A sixties cult TV series, starring Patrick McGoohan.
[3] Kieron has toured extensively with The Prodigy. He's just a bit more experienced than us!

but for now each of us needs to assemble our own rig. The act before us is in full swing, and the sound levels are uncomfortably high, so I put earphones in my ears to keep the noise down.

One thing I've not predicted is the absolute lack of light. Mark's to my left, busy plugging in cables. He's got a torch. I'm not that organised and have to feel my way to the right sockets. This is all new to us; the lack of time, the lack of light, the feeling that this bunch of older citizens might be better off having a nice cup of tea somewhere. The previous band has finished their set, and the stage has been cleared. It's time for us to be wheeled on[4]. There's no power supply in the wings, so this is the first opportunity to check that the gear works. And that's what we're doing now.

The audience is streaming in. There's a smell of grass, sweat, and canvas. The wind's rattling the sides of the marquee, which does nothing to dispel the feeling that we are in the middle of a field. We're a very long way from Maida Vale. I can't spend hours tinkering with the gear. What happens in the next 45 minutes is it.

We launch into the opening number, 'Till the Lights Go Out'. Doing something new right up front seems like a good idea. We don't want to be our own tribute band, but somehow the lyrics seem worryingly appropriate...

> *You think you're kind of hip*
> *But you're really not*
> *You really think you're cool*
> *But you're not that hot*
> *You think you've got it all*
> *But it's not a lot*
> *You really have to*
> *Hold on to what you've got*
> *Till the lights go out*

---

[4] An unfortunate turn of phrase. I meant the equipment of course, not us.

It goes down well. There seems to be a genuine warmth from the audience, and more are joining all the time.

Things are going swimmingly but we run into problems. All the synthesisers and sounds need to change instantly, sometimes in the middle of a number, and it's a big ask. About half way through the set, Mark's computer decides that it's too big and crashes.

This is our first gig and we're in that nightmare scenario of standing on a stage with nothing to do. It's at times like these that everyone should have Dick Mills on hand. He immediately takes the house mike and starts chatting to the audience.

Of course, for them, this could be part of the act, seeing us playing around with vintage synthesisers, trying to get things to work. It's an image of the Radiophonic Workshop which emerged out of the austere and disciplined BBC of the nineteen fifties.

Early Days

Back then, the simplicity of the studios had surprised me.

Like a scene from a Somerset Maugham short story, here in Broadcasting House there were many studios that contained one table, one microphone, and two chairs, their control rooms having a record player, a tape recorder, and a four channel mixer. Although linear faders had appeared in a lot of the newer studios, BBC Radio Schools were still using old post-war mixing desks. There was little opportunity to change the sound.

The BBC saw its role in the early days as a mouthpiece for the performance of others. A way for the great and the good, those with something worthwhile to say, to reach their public. It was not there to tamper with the content, but to faithfully reproduce it and transmit it; anything else would be a distortion.

They placed little value in their employees being creative from the ground up; any ideas they had that were born without the initial input of a so-called 'contributor' were often ignored. This was not a callous disregard for the talents of their workforce, but a simple recognition of what the BBC was expected to do.

Imagine then, the sort of reception Daphne Oram and Desmond Briscoe received, when they embarked on a project that was specifically designed to encourage original thought: the Radiophonic Workshop.

By 1970, the BBC stood at a crossroads. To be honest, the BBC was such a massive institution, and getting it to turn the corner into a new age such an undertaking, that different bits of it often stood at a crossroads. It took many years for newer studio equipment to appear in radio studios that were in constant use. I remember many live Radio 4 shows using desks with rotary knobs to control the sound. The first linear[5] fader I ever saw was in a news studio, shortly before joining the Radiophonic Workshop. Gradually, though, more up-to-date equipment came on stream, delighting the newer recruits but confusing many older members of staff. These were people whose experience was different from mine. People who, despite sharing the same job title, had different attitudes, experience, and skills. It was a fascinating insight into the BBC that had existed before I was born, a lot of which still remained.

Take the Langham for instance. Today, The Langham Hotel opposite Broadcasting House is the go-to destination for anyone willing to spend a minimum of £450 a night for a room in the heart of London. Back then, its somewhat tatty exterior hid a maze of half glazed partitions and endless linoleum. It resembled a giant dentist's waiting room. The only evidence of its Victorian glory days was the elegant staircase winding around two wonderful elevators, a lift operator in each. I always marvelled at the dedication of these men and women in their faded uniforms. For them, working for such an august institution as the BBC was reward

---

[5] One that travels vertically.

enough. Every day, they would take me to the third floor of the building, where I was training to become a Studio Manager. Below us, on the second floor, there were rooms set aside for staff who needed to stay over before their shifts the next day. In 1973, shortly before I left for Maida Vale, a Radio 2 announcer named James Alexander Gordon saw the top half of a silver-haired Victorian gentleman with a cloak and cravat moving across his bedroom floor; the man's legs appeared embedded in the carpet. They later discovered that the level of the floor had changed in one of the refurbishments and the ghostly figure was walking on a floor that was no longer there[6].

The BBC Club was on the eastern side of the building, on the ground floor. A doorman oversaw its smoke-filled rooms. His main duty was to answer the telephone and summon people out of the alcoholic haze when they needed to take a call. His devotion to duty was unwavering. Pranksters would leave spoof messages asking for people that didn't exist. Charles Prince, Michael Mouse, and even on one occasion, Ben Nevis. Without flinching, he would carefully relay the messages over the tannoy.

My work as a Studio Manager in Broadcasting House covered several networks, but was mostly Radio 4. We operated the studios for a wide range of broadcasts: news, sport, drama, speech, live magazine programmes, but, sadly, few music shows. Assignments in classical music, for channels such as BBC Radio 3, were only accessible to Studio Managers with a music degree, and the ability to sight read scores. It was a rarefied world, similar to Glyndebourne Opera House where, ironically, I'd worked before joining the BBC.

Many of the programmes of that period are still running today: **You and Yours, Today, World at One, PM, Desert Island Discs** and **Woman's Hour**. We became very adept at using the equipment, plugging up studios and playing tapes and vinyl into programmes. So, the emphasis was more on the producing of programme material rather than engineering; a skill

---

[6] Absolutely nothing to do with my story but an irresistible tale, nonetheless.

that was to be an essential quality for anyone wishing to work at the Radiophonic Workshop. Except for the last composer to work there, Richard Attree, we'd all started as Studio Managers or Engineers in radio.

It was when I was playing recorded tapes into these programmes that I noticed blue leader for the first time. Leader, in this context, was plastic tape, often yellow in colour, that was unable to record sound, but was instead used to separate portions of recording with silence. It also acted as a cue point for playing in the recorded material. In Broadcasting House, blue leader was a rarity, but when it did appear, you couldn't help but notice the quality and originality of the material that followed. Eventually I had to ask.

"Ah, that stuff's from the Radiophonic Workshop," came the reply.

At the time, I'd never touched a synthesiser and couldn't really see how my musical background writing songs and instrumentals would qualify me for a job there. Besides, I had no knowledge of this strange department, apart from its connection with the **Doctor Who** title music, but whenever that blue leader appeared I paid special attention.

I remember the first time I played the title music to the arts programme, **Kaleidoscope**, for instance. It was clean, pitch perfect, and unlike anything I'd heard before. I later learned that this strikingly direct and modern music was Paddy Kingsland's trade mark. Seen from the perspective of the humdrum, sparsely equipped studios of Broadcasting House, this Radiophonic Workshop was literally something else.

In the end, it was an unconnected event that would kick start my journey towards BBC Maida Vale.

My nostalgia for amateur dramatics had led me to join 'Ariel', the BBC's non-professional theatre group. None of their output was ever broadcast, but they did stage annual shows at the Lamda Theatre in Earls Court, and the Cockpit Theatre in Paddington. It was in the Cockpit that I had my first taste of electronic music.

A small group of Ariel members had got together to present shows devised around a particular theme, and asked me to provide some music for 'Seaplay', a show about sea and seafaring. One of the group, who was a talented artist and storyteller, had painted some pictures which told the story of Solomenti, a plucky little fish, who despite his enthusiasm for life, was 'very worried about the international situation'. This was the late seventies and the cold war served as a rather sombre background to everything. We were all 'very worried about the international situation'.

We decided to make photo slides of each of the paintings and project them onto the backcloth, together with an appropriate soundtrack.

A discussion ensued about the style of music that would fit this rather tongue-in-cheek story of life beneath the waves. Somebody suggested electronic sounds. By coincidence, as we were discussing this, a member of the Cockpit theatre staff was walking across the back of the stage, and overheard the conversation.

"We've got a few bits and pieces upstairs that might interest you," he said. "The room up there gets used for youth groups and they've got quite a lot of gear. Have a look. Use whatever you want. Just as long as you don't remove it."

Two of us climbed the stairs at the side of the stage, and pushed open the door into a large space, full of a variety of props and packing boxes, and there, sitting amongst them, were three VCS3 synthesisers[7].

We plugged one of them into the mains and started to experiment. On the table alongside, there was a brief guide. It showed how to plug the tiny switchboard matrix with a selection of pins to get your first sound.

---

[7] One of them was advertised on eBay in 2012 for $12,000. They are now much sought after beasts.

I'd played around with an oscillator mounted on a small printed circuit board in my studio in Hove; these sounds were similar but you could perform and modify them. The VCS3 seemed like an ideal sound source for Solomenti's music.

There was a logistical problem, however. We wanted to make a soundtrack to go with the projections, and yet these synthesisers were not allowed to leave the room in the Cockpit Theatre. The only solution was to bring the recording apparatus to the synthesiser. These days, that would hardly be a problem, but then, I used a Revox 736 tape recorder[8]. It was a heavy brute, and hardly portable without injury, but undeterred we dragged it up the stairs to record my first piece of electronic music. It was primitive stuff, but the audience seemed to enjoy it, if only because these were truly new sounds.

After the two performances, we gathered for the inevitable after-show party, and discussion turned to the music that accompanied the paintings. There was a lot of interest in the synthesisers I'd used, and somebody said: *"You know, you should join the Radiophonic Workshop."*

---

[8] I still have the machine in my garage, and use it if I have need to play the original tapes of my early pre-BBC material.

BBC6 Music

Old Haunts

The Radiophonic Workshop band is playing for BBC 6 Music tonight at BBC Maida Vale. It's December 16th, 2013.

I worked for 24 years in this building and haven't been back since 1998, when the Workshop closed and I left the BBC.

It's home to a variety of departments and has hosted broadcasts and recording sessions since 1934, when the BBC Symphony Orchestra took up residence. To this day, when the orchestra's in this building, BBC Maida Vale feels complete.

They're not here today. In fact, the place is like an abandoned outpost with little activity. I'm no longer greeted by a commissionaire who knows me, but one who suspects I have no right to be there. Luckily, guest passes have been left for us and his mood softens. It all seems different, but the changes are superficial.

Framed pictures of conductors hang on the walls, reminding me of an old guesthouse that can't wait to show off the celebrities that have stayed there. Under the pictures are elderly sofas looking for some action. They've clearly seen a lot, but a long time ago.

The commissionaire's cheerful now, but resigned. Does he realise that he's sitting on the balcony where they used to serve teas?

Way back when the building was new, it was home to the Maida Vale Skating Palace and Club, and around its long left side was a balcony at ground floor level. It overlooked the rink below, half of which is now the orchestral studio.

This balcony housed the Radiophonic Workshop and, to its right, a long corridor still runs the length of the building, with a wall separating it from the orchestral studio.

I have to unload the gear from my car. I grab my pass and head outside. I can see our Transit van up at Door B, halfway down the length of the building. There's a goods lift inside the door that feeds straight down to the lower level, and we trundle the flight cases along the familiar corridors towards Studio 3.

On our left, is the rather sad rest area stranded in a windowless island; on our right, the toilets. One night, I recorded the sound of an operatic soprano here. The toilets were empty but there was a draught escaping from the air conditioning, filtered by a slightly open door[1].

We wheel further down the corridor and into another wider area. The public entrance to the building used for live concerts.

One further set of doors, and we are in our studio for today. It's changed little since I was last in the building. Sessions for Radio 2 and jazz concerts have always taken place here; in fact there's a plaque commemorating

---

[1] I still have the sample made from this sound. It's called 'Dorwind'.

Bing Crosby's last recording above the window into the control room, where we can see two studio managers preparing for the session.

We're playing live tonight into Marc Riley's show on BBC 6 Music, being broadcast from Salford in Manchester. The music will be relayed via this local control room, and there'll be a chance to chat with Marc down the line.

We've decided to play three numbers live, and record another for later broadcast.

Paddy Kingsland's 'Vespucci' goes well, and for a simple reason. We can all see the drummer. The studio is huge, bigger than any stage we've played on, and with the absence of a live audience we've set up in a circle.

'Incubus' by Roger Limb is very much an ensemble piece which we're used to playing, but the final number based on a poem is less familiar. In fact, this will be the first time it's been heard.

The Workshop was always known for its unusual treatments of poetry (an early rendition of 'Private Dreams and Public Nightmares' attracted a lot of attention at the time, and there have been many more over the years) but up to now, this type of number has been missing from our repertoire. Following a trawl through the internet we came across Peter Adam Salomon's poem, 'Electricity and Language and Me'.

The text is ideal for Radiophonic treatment, and we weave live electronic sounds around the words, spoken by the DJ Andrew Weatherall. His voice is being added to our performance from a pre-recorded track.

Our fourth item just has to be **Doctor Who**. In concert, we now finish our set with a seven minute version that builds from Delia's music, and finishes with my 1980 version.

The session goes OK, and despite being hundreds of miles apart, so do the chats with Marc Riley. Eventually, we say our goodbyes and begin packing up.

It's an odd experience. In a concert, there's a beginning, a middle and an end. Tonight, there have been what feels like three middles. Three performances followed by a sudden switching off and leaving.

In stage concerts, it's clear who's been listening and what they think of it, but after a broadcast, feedback's far harder to come by. The only certainty is that the production crew have heard your music; the rest of the audience, potentially numbered in millions, remains unknown.

The gear gets ferried past the lonely rest area, where there's now a solitary musician taking a break. Probably an escapee from the rock studios close by. Corridors can be desolate places in BBC buildings. No sound can escape the acoustic isolation of each studio, and there's a sense of 'missing out', sitting there with your head bowed over a cup of machine tea.

I need to return my visitor's pass to the Reception, up on the ground floor. Rather than go out to the street, I climb the familiar back stairs and head along the top corridor, once home to the Radiophonic Workshop, counting down the rooms on my right.

Thirteen, twelve, eleven…

Attached

There had been a good deal of smoking going on in Room 11.

This was John Baker's studio, and he sat on a high stool in front of one of the three Philips tape machines holding a razor blade and a loop of 1/4 inch recording tape.

The smell of cigarettes mixed with another aroma. Hard to pin down at first, but when a tiny puppy trotted out from behind the speaker, all became clear.

"I'm not supposed to have him here, so don't mention it, will you?" He set about slicing the tape in an editing block. "He pees everywhere, it's a nightmare."

This was my first day on attachment to the Radiophonic Workshop, and I was already being given more responsibility than I could handle.

There were bits of tape everywhere. Hanging on the wall, dangling from the side of the tape machine, held on with sticky tape. I was impressed with the speed he worked. Splicing tape in the editing block, attaching it to another piece, and then back into the main reel so he could play the result.

Painters or sculptors have always worked alone, but till the advent of recorded audio, composers had to rely on musicians to interpret their scores. It was only with the coming of tape recording that it was possible for a composer, with some knowledge of the technology, to create a whole piece from scratch. There was something immediately satisfying about seeing him work. This was not just a musical skill.

It was clear that I had a lot to learn.

The Workshop I discovered that morning was not at the forefront of technology. It had no budget, no money of its own, and had become a living store cupboard full of hand-me-downs, and occasional presents from rich uncles[2].

On one of the shelves in John's studio stood a couple of Test Oscillators from BBC Engineering. Cumbersome metal boxes with one large control

---

[2] This was the era of patronage, where occasional gifts were bestowed on the department.

to change the pitch of a sine wave. Was this used to make the 'Ooo eee Ooo' in Delia Derbyshire's iconic piece?

During my first few years in the Corporation, almost everything was in mono[3].

The fact that humans have two ears was something that had not escaped the notice of early BBC engineers, but they had enough trouble getting the sound to come out of one speaker cleanly, without making their lives unnecessarily complicated[4]. Besides, around the time of the BBC's first experimental broadcasts in stereo in 1962, there were plenty of people in the industry who claimed that you could be more inventive in mono. One of them exclaimed that the arrival of stereo made him feel blind, because he could no longer imagine a scene in his head, but was forced to hear it in front of him, and then only six foot wide.

Even when the BBC officially declared itself as broadcasting classical music in stereo on the Third Programme[5], it was very patchy on other networks. And so it was in the Radiophonic Workshop, where stereo facilities were few and far between.

It's tempting to think of the department as a large open room lined with racks of strange devices, loops and electronics, with earnest creators, perhaps in white coats, tending the machines. Of course, that would be impractical. All the sounds would compete.

No, this was a series of small rooms down the left-hand side of a very long corridor. I left John Baker to his work, and pushed open the next door.

---

[3] A one channel, one speaker system.
[4] In fact, they had been experimenting with it for years but were rolling it out slowly.
[5] Today's Radio 3.

Room 12 was full of stuff. Unwanted tables, filing cabinets and shelves, machines and bits of gear; all picked up from across BBC Radio. Everything was perched on something else: scripts, papers, tape boxes and somebody's discarded coat. Strange sprung levers fixed onto metal stands, a long thin transparent plastic tube that increased in size along its length, with a tiny loudspeaker in its base. You felt as if you'd stumbled off the highway into someone's attic room. There was even a hot water tank over in the corner, by a Levers Rich tape machine, and a strange box called a Tempophon[6]. Beside them, a tower spewing jack leads from row upon row of sockets.

The predominant colour was a grey green, only relieved by the most sci-fi piece of equipment in the room, the polished wood and white fascia of a VCS3 synthesiser, an array of knobs on its surface, its LFO light flashing red[7].

Nine years had elapsed since two VCS3 synthesisers had arrived in 1965. Regarded by some as usurpers, they were versatile replacements for the test oscillators of the past, but capable of doing a lot more.

In 1970, the company that made the VCS3 had delivered a much larger version—many VCS3s in one box, and a lot more besides. This Synthi 100 stood in Room 10, behind a locked door. I remember walking along this corridor as a Studio Manager and standing to listen outside. There was a muted discussion between two people, followed by a strange chattering sound that seemed to be the opening and closing of a mouth. A pause, and then the discussion started again, followed by a distant echo. I imagined this to be a deep mysterious space, but the truth was less exciting. The door opened onto a dark, pokey little room, with a small window onto the street outside. Traffic passed along Delaware Road in front of the staid Victorian mansion flats. There was a large piece of

---

[6] It had a revolving tape head which, together with speed change, could change pitch without speed. I once used it to make "Hallelujah" sing in a different key. The quality was terrible.

[7] This scene has since inspired the cover of our recent release, *Burials in Several Earths*.

furniture along the right-hand side that was only properly revealed when the lights were on. The Synthi 100 had a vast array of knobs spread over its top panels, with two enormous matrices on the lower half, dotted with coloured pins. Illuminated numbers shone out over the controls of a step sequencer, and in front, stood a keyboard. That this monolithic synthesiser occupied the same department as the copper water tank was difficult to imagine. I really was standing at the crossroads between two ages.

I was on a three month attachment to the department[8]. Three months to make an impression and hopefully apply for a job. I was excited, and a little daunted at the same time. Could I follow the illustrious history that had gone before? That so-called Golden Age which had produced such ground-breaking work, despite the limitations of the equipment.

As I have said, everything had been in mono. Material was recorded on reel-to-reel tape, which generated hiss. Even the individual pieces of gear resulted in noise. Anything containing valves, and there were a lot of those, emitted a lot of heat and a great deal of hum. So hiss and hum were the enemies of early recordings, and the Radiophonic Workshop spent a large amount of time every day trying to remove them.

This pre-occupation with hiss forced composers of early electro-acoustic music to 'roll off the top', to filter out all the top frequencies. Their audience heard the resulting plummy sound as a creative choice, when it was often a technical necessity. Delia Derbyshire's **Doctor Who** theme features many of those filtered sounds. In those days, each musical line was recorded onto a different piece of tape and could have its top removed separately. The 'Dum dee Dum' and the 'Ooo eee Ooo' lack top, but the whoosh-like white noise is left untreated and supplies the higher frequencies.

Whatever the technical limitations, these were iconic pieces that still

---

[8] From January to March 1974.

resonate today, and represent a high point in the Workshop's history and a time of intense creativity.

There was no chance that I could match their unique work, but some of the original composers had taken an instant dislike to the new technology, so there might be an opening for someone willing to take it on. But even then, I wouldn't be the first to do so. Paddy Kingsland had embraced this new equipment and was working in the next room on a programme for the TV series, **Horizon**.

Thanks to the success of Delia's **Doctor Who**, the Workshop was getting more and more commissions from television. His studio, Room 13, was an environment I'd get used to, with a mixer, more keyboards, and a guitar propped up in the corner.

He was adjusting the sound on an ARP Odyssey synthesiser[9]. It had been purchased in the early seventies, and was delivering some full electronic sounds which made the VCS3 sound rather thin.

There was a real feeling of experimentation about every room in the Workshop. The composers were like miners panning for gold, confident that an exciting new sound was just a moment away. I couldn't wait to get started.

Desmond Briscoe, the head of the Workshop, was apprehensive about letting me cut my teeth on anything too high profile, and looking at a list of my early work, his apprehension is only too obvious.

Here are the entries from the Radiophonic Library Catalogue (taken from Mark Ayres' Database, which he created from the original records).

---

[9] He had used the ARP to create the **Kaleidoscope** music I had so admired as a studio manager.

Composer	Peter Howell	TRW No.7936
Title	**Let's Join In: Some Pie in the Sky**	
Producer	Colin Smith	
Department	Features, Arts & Education	
Requirement Service	Radio 4	

I can easily dismiss this first entry; the sound of a flying steak and kidney pie. Not really one for the album, and a rather ignominious start.

Composer	Peter Howell	TRW No.7936
Title	**Bus Timetable Alteration Ident.**	
Series	Radio Brighton	
Producer	Bob Gunnell (Station Manager)	
Department	Radio Brighton	
Requirement Service	Local Radio	
Company Notes	Report in Box.	

A bicycle bell and a forgettable synthesiser riff for Radio Brighton's *Traffic News*. Did the job, but didn't set the world alight.

Composer	Peter Howell	TRW No.7938
Title	**Quest: Gilgamesh**	
Series	Quest	
Producer	Geoffrey Curtis	
Department	Features, Arts & Education	
Requirement Service	Radio 4	

A mixture of sound and music used in the retelling of an ancient myth from Persia about the creation of the world. A bit more to this, and a chance to play around with some epic sounds. This was my first experience in writing music for a drama and I tackled **Gilgamesh** with great enthusiasm. It was well received, but suffered from being too literal, reflecting events in the drama but adding nothing new. One cue, I remember, was a magic waterfall achieved by echoing a set of descending notes on a VCS3 using several tape machines and different speeds. This was nine years after the arrival of the first synths, and we were still using hybrid techniques, because there were no other means of engineering the sounds that we needed.

Composer	Peter Howell	TRW No.7972
Title	The Glass Lady	
Series		
Producer	Colin Smith	
Department	Features, Arts & Education	
Requirement Service	Radio 4	
Company Notes	Excerpts on PH-DAT.	

The sound of a witch's greenhouse collapsing.

This fourth item, which on the face of it was no more exciting than the flying pie, would kick start my interest in creating something original. It allowed me to try John Baker's famous technique of recording sounds at different pitches onto tape, cutting the tape to note lengths and sticking them back together as a series of pitches. I used the sound of a glass pane being struck as it's lowered into water[10], gave it a skewed pitch, and re-recorded the result at different pitches. These were then re-assembled as a downward cascade. The recording of that cascade was then repeated, in

---

[10] I used these sounds again in my score for the **Doctor Who** adventure, *Kinda*.

overlapping and ever descending runs.

I found the result exciting. The technology had somehow made it greater than the sounds it contained. This was my first experience of two plus two equals five, and I couldn't wait for it to happen again.

There was a lot of wide-eyed innocence at work here. I'd only just started, and all I could muster were limited skills and experiences from my pre-BBC days.

I'd been composing music since I was about fourteen years old[11]. By the time I joined the BBC, I'd written over a hundred pieces, many songs but also, crucially, many more instrumentals. It was these, inspired by my interest in The Shadows[12], that would provide my early harmony lessons and a fascination with arrangements and orchestration. I've always enjoyed finding things out for myself. Sadly, that makes me a terrible student[13].

Suspicious of imposed rules, I set off on a voyage of personal but isolated discovery. When I should have been studying music in the conventional way, I was experimenting in an unconventional way. This process led to a musical life set aside from those who had followed the true path.

I remain to this day rather bad at a lot of music-related skills. My keyboard and guitar playing skills are very idiosyncratic, because ideas have always controlled everything. I have an idea and then set about teaching myself just enough to be able to see it through. It's a strange way to accumulate

---

[11] In fact, I had been writing plays and stories since the age of ten, and hadn't considered music until discovering an aptitude for the guitar.
[12] For the record, I was never a Cliff Richard fan, in fact didn't like his songs at all. This made looking at *Summer Holiday* a stop-start affair affair. I was only interested in the instrumentals by the Shadows.
[13] I had to confess this to all my new students at The National Film and Television School, where I lectured after leaving the BBC. Ironic, but true.

expertise, and it didn't pass me any exams, but over the years I seem to have amassed enough[14].

My early experience was shaped by a partnership with another music enthusiast. John Ferdinando played bass in a band I was in, and lived with his parents in Hassocks ,Sussex. We frequently used his parents' house for rehearsals. At one of these, John mentioned that a local amateur drama group was working on an adaptation of Lewis Carroll's *Alice Through the Looking Glass* and were looking for some music. I'd been writing some Shadows-style instrumentals for the band and had taken to producing demos of the numbers on a tape recorder. John became interested in recording, and in early 1968 we started to experiment.

Composing the music for *Alice* provided us with two things that have become the mainstay of my career ever since: the feeling of being wanted, and a deadline. If John Ferdinando had forgotten to mention that the Ditchling Players needed a composer, I really wonder if all this would have happened.

The production proved popular, and we decided to try to sell a few LPs of the music. First of all, we needed to find someone to transfer our recordings to vinyl. The company we chose had a lower limit of fifty pressings and we only knew about twenty people who might want to buy one. We reluctantly agreed, but the whole thing seemed rash and a waste of money.

Today original copies of this album can fetch in excess of £1000[15]. Our concern over people's lack of interest had the reverse effect. The thing has become a rarity, and collectors love that.

Despite its limited immediate sales, John and I'd become hooked on the

---

[14] Of course, it's diametrically opposed to academic music teaching, where you acquire a set of recognised skills first and then see how you can apply them.
[15] These sales between collectors don't result in any money coming back to John and myself, and so we can only look on and wonder.

idea of producing albums. We made four more through a partnership called 'H&F Recordings'. It was a varied collection, if only because we changed the name of the band for each one! *Tomorrow Come Someday*, which was music for an amateur film, *Fly Away*, an album that others have labelled 'psychedelic folk', a wonderful solo album by John Ferdinando, *A Game for All Who Know*, and a solo album of mine called *Friends*. This was made during my early years at the BBC, and features a studio manager colleague of mine, Ruth Cubbin, on several tracks. All five albums are now collectables, and all five were engineered in a rather peculiar way.

When we started work on *Alice Through the Looking Glass* in my parents' house in Hove, John Ferdinando and I used a Revox Tape Machine (the semi pro arm of Studer). On this stereo machine, you could record something on the top track, and then play that back to the bottom track whilst adding something new. With a little dexterity and forward planning, you built up some really intricate tracks. Our first two albums, *Alice Through the Looking Glass* and *Tomorrow Come Someday* were created this way. After that, we used to bounce in stereo in between two Revox machines, but the idea was the same; the gradual evolution of a full track. We created another three albums using that technique.

Dovetailed into the production of those albums were five stage shows written by John and myself through our own small and very amateur business, 'Whizz Theatre Company'. Very creatively busy times.

During my first days at the Workshop, I was only too aware of what had led me there, and I wondered whether it was going to be enough. After all, there was a frightening difference between what I'd been doing to date and what I was now expected to do.

While in my studio in Hove, writing songs and instrumentals, I was effectively working for myself, now suddenly and for the next 26 years, I would be working for somebody else. It was their requirements and their films and programmes that would dictate what was needed, not me.

It came as a terrible shock. Every item of music[16] could only come about after an initial discussion with a producer or director. It was always their brief that kickstarted the work.

So, another layer was added to the creative process. All those ideas that came so easily had to be passed through an initial filter that removed everything that was unsuitable for the project in hand. Sometimes there wasn't much left.

Listening to my early work at the Workshop, you can't help noticing the desperate use of skills that I felt safe with. The acoustic steel string guitar featured somewhere in a lot of things, the use of any percussion from any source, roughly recorded.

People who came to the Workshop on attachment expected to take to it immediately, but were sometimes taken aback by how much time was spent on their own. The isolation was compounded by having to know enough about the gear to coax something new and appropriate from it. I was jumping in the deep end, but luckily help was at hand. Paddy Kingsland introduced me to the wonders of click tracks, the workings of the multitrack recorders and a lot else besides.

The Radiophonic Workshop was a radio department, and radio was proud to have us under its wing, but there were tensions. The BBC must have looked like a large monolithic organisation from the outside, but suffered from internal rivalries of all sorts. Individual programmes were in competition. When I was a Studio Manager working on the news programme **PM**, I was sent down to Broadcasting House reception, to meet an interviewee. The guest was quite a catch and everyone wanted to hear from him. By the time I made it downstairs, the man had been poached by someone working on *The World at One*, who had spotted him in the foyer. When the producers of **PM** complained, they were shocked to find out that the interview had already been broadcast live.

---

[16] Clearly, this does not include music for homegrown specials such as *The Inferno*.

On a larger scale, there was a long running gulf between the world of television and radio, and a palpable sense of 'them and us'. Radio occupied the BBC's original purpose-built home, and the staff in radio looked down their noses at Television Centre[17]. So, it came as a terrible shock to BBC Radio management when Desmond Briscoe said he had been approached by a Television Producer.

The Workshop's unusual output had come to the notice of Verity Lambert. She was making a new science fiction series for BBC1 and wanted the Radiophonic Workshop to be involved.

Doctor Who put the Workshop on the map, and through some careful negotiation on Desmond Briscoe's part, the name of the department appeared on the closing credits of every episode. This was no longer word of mouth. I, and countless others sitting at home watching the programmes, started wondering what this place could be, and what curious procedures could create these sounds.

---

[17] Despite hiding a slight envy and excitement at the thought of 'doing TV'.

Cecil Sharp House

The Smell of Apples

We're playing at Cecil Sharp House tonight.

There have been many occasions when our presence at festivals has seemed incongruous on paper, but turns out to be spot on, on the night. This is one of those; a band full of synthesisers playing in the home of British folk. We arrive during the day, and the place is everything you would expect. Someone's practicing the banjo, leaning against a wall in the entrance, and as we drag our equipment through the foyer, we can hear the strains of an accordion band running through a few jigs.

This is the home of the English Folk Dance and Song Society, and the Vaughan Williams Memorial Library, containing a lot of his original scores. I have an abiding love of his music and his presence is intensely felt in this building. I was associated with folk music in my early days, but a rather irreverent version that became known as 'psychedelic folk'. I had nothing to do with the label, but I suppose plucked steel string guitars, vocals, electronics and tape manipulation do need a category of their own.

In the large, impressive hall there's a modest stage. Just about big enough for us, although Kieron our drummer will end up sitting on a ledge at the back of the hall, as there's not enough depth to accommodate his drum stool.

Off to the right, perched on some packing cases, someone is picking at a steel string guitar and singing a traditional song. His voice has an amazing clarity. Makes you want to drop everything and stop and listen. Months later, when I'm wandering through the crowds at the Green Man Festival in Wales, the same guy will come up to me to say hello. I never cease to be amazed at the variety of people who take an interest in the Radiophonic Workshop. It has come as a genuine surprise to all of us.

We shoe horn our gear onto the stage. Cosy but not impossible, although Mark and I are concerned that every time I stand up, all of his gear moves down by a few inches. We run through a couple of numbers for the soundcheck and take a break before the evening's performance.

During this time, two things become clear about the gig. Firstly, we are not the only performers on the bill. There will be acoustic sets from a variety of musicians, and even half an hour of line dancing. Two elderly ladies playing fiddles and a male accordionist are rehearsing for that in a side room. Secondly, the vast majority of the audience will be drunk. During the afternoon, a wide variety of ciders (almost nothing else but cider) becomes available in the two cafes downstairs. Chatter becomes more animated, and the air smells of apples. In this alcoholic haze, success will be guaranteed. Although a determined reviewer, drinking nothing but sparkling water, could still tell the world what it was really like.

The line dancers are doing their thing, and we are up next.

It's an intimate stage. Not very high, and so the front row of the audience is close. In fact, so close that during the show, you feel as if you're forming some sort of special bond with them.

Over the months, I've been getting to grips with playing the Akai EWI Wind Controller. It's a clarinet-like instrument that has a USB connection to the gear and allows you to play and use breath control on any synthesiser or sampler sound. Tonight, I'm playing it on quite a few numbers, and I'm apprehensive. My nervousness is compounded by two young women on the front row who have spotted the instrument in its stand (actually it's upright in a large jar. Very folksy). They clearly know what it is and are discussing it. As the evening progresses, I convince myself that either one of these women can play it a lot better than me. They even make eye contact and look down at the instrument; it's getting tense.

Thanks to a great deal of goodwill on their part, and the cider induced alcoholic haze, it goes well; they've clearly had a great time.

We set about derigging the gear. Out it goes through the foyer again, into the waiting Transit van. As I'm wheeling yet another flight case across the hall, the two elderly ladies from the line dancing band are coming down the stairs. I'm not expecting them to talk to me.

"*We really enjoyed that,*" they said. "*It was worth staying for.*"

Life in the Long Nissan Hut

The final consumers of our music were hard to visualise, gathered around their TVs, unaware of the dark corridors of the BBC at Delaware Road in Maida Vale. It is still there, in the listed building[1]. An honour bestowed on it for its art deco facade that runs down the entire length. As you look up, the effect is shattered by a corrugated iron roof that also runs

---

[1] At the time of writing anyway. The BBC has announced that it will be selling the Maida Vale building and moving its activities to a new centre in Shoreditch.

down the entire length. This split personality is continued in the interior, where its weak attempt at 1970s design is only ever a flimsy wall away from the true bowels of the building. A large cavern of receding pipes, Escher-like staircases and dark voids cover the whole outer perimeter at basement level. Those of you that remember the last scene of *The Poseidon Adventure* (the original, with Gene Hackman) will know what I mean. There are giant brick boxes, each of which is a studio. Enormous 40ft cubes with 20ft of air in between. Now that really is sound insulation.

It's a low building, with most of its content below ground. The original Radiophonic Workshop occupied a few rooms at the front of the building, but later expanded inwards and away from the light.

Most people working in BBC Maida Vale do so in windowless rooms. For about 22 of my 26 years at the Workshop, I was one of those. It was a wonder I didn't get rickets. I worked long hours, and in winter, would go to work in the dark and come home in the dark.

Where possible though, we would all repair to the canteen at lunchtime. After an hour or so, back we would go to our studios to pick up where we left off. Sometimes though, the moment would have passed, and the thought we were having at 12.45 seemed irrelevant at 2.30. We should have stayed till it was finished, and then gone to lunch, because the equipment had no means of memorising the settings. Any tampering while you were away would be a disaster. Until it was committed to tape, you could only be sure of what was happening at that instant. We should have been Buddhists.

I got particularly worried about this technical amnesia in the middle of a large project when I left the studio overnight. To have a record of the settings, I would crawl around the floor with a cassette recorder, describing the position of every knob. Those recordings must exist somewhere, but I wouldn't rush to listen to them again!

Though the Workshop was strung out along a long corridor, there were a few studios up a small offshoot towards the centre of the building. My room, Studio B, was quite a walk from the Workshop office. It's a solitary job and a sudden contrast can often kick start an idea, so I've never had a problem with being disturbed. The Head of the Radiophonic Workshop, Brian Hodgson must have realised this, and suggested that all important visitors should come along to my studio. Sometimes these visits would happen with little warning, the door swinging open to reveal the UK Head of Yamaha, or on one occasion Melvyn Bragg. To add to my discombobulation[2], a conversation that would have started on their way down the corridor, continued unabated in my studio. I joined in out of politeness, but with no idea what we were talking about.

The walk to the canteen down that long corridor was always eventful. Artists and contributors used it as a shortcut from the studios downstairs, and I often found I was accompanying well known actors or singers.

I was always struck by the strange world of top classical singers. In many works, there would be four soloists: soprano, contralto, tenor, and bass. When they broke for lunch, all four of them would set off towards the canteen. A rather high pitched screechy one, a rather sinister lower pitched one, a guy whose voice had broken but only just, and one whose speech was so low, it rattled. And wherever each of them went, whoever they were singing with, they would always find themselves with three similar companions. Following them to the canteen, and hearing the bass ask for a Spanish Omelette with the voice of doom, brought a smile to your face.

We all did it. Brian Hodgson and Delia Derbyshire were both busy working on a piece in one of the Radiophonic studios and heard that Karlheinz Stockhausen was in the building rehearsing a piece. They followed him to the canteen, expecting him to have prearranged some unique meal to match his special status, only to overhear him asking for

---

[2] Thanks, **Blackadder**.

Savoury Mince.

Before you reached Reception and the canteen, there were two very special doors with small glass windows in the top. They looked onto the balcony of Studio 1 and the large orchestral space below. I'm pleased to say that I've spied on a great number of internationally famous conductors and heard them rehearsing and recording an amazing variety of music, including every Proms performance by the BBC Symphony Orchestra. Spending each day designing the sounds we were making, it was good to see what dizzying heights you can reach using instruments that have already been invented!

The relentless flow of work took me by surprise; and the variety of projects too. TV and Radio shows would coexist and composing was taking place on several jobs at once.

The variety of work was impressive.

Choice for Tomorrow	February 1975	TV Continuing Education	BBC1
Answers to Listeners' Questions	February 1975	English by Radio	External Services
Stories and Rhymes: Warrior Princess	February 1975	Features, Art & Education	Radio 4
Merry-Go-Round: Series Ident	March 1975	TV Schools	BBC1
In Service	April 1975	Talks	Radio 4
Pila-Pila	April 1975	Childrens' Wales	Regional Television

Discovery: Beginners	May 1975	Features, Art & Education	Radio 4 Schools
English by Radio: Teaching Observed	May 1975	English by Radio	External Services
Doctor Who (Serial 4H): Planet of Evil	June 1975	Drama	BBC1 Effects
Space for Man	June 1975	Arts and Features	BBC1

Merry-Go-Round, which aptly described the whole job, was a short piece played in one pass on the ARP Odyssey, but with some syncopated echoes from a tape delay.

I even stood in for Dick Mills doing the effects on the **Doctor Who** adventure, *Planet of Evil*. Although, it would be a long while before I got another bite at that cherry.

Then there was *Space for Man*[3] for TV, my first experience of scoring for live musicians. The session was held in one of the downstairs studios. It was not a runaway success, my conducting skills having proved inadequate, and the music I'd composed was disappointing. The programme, a television special for the Arts and Features department, revealed how exciting new satellite technology would transform our lives. It was funded by many European broadcasters, and so had plenty of money to spend on the music.

Little did I know that this was the first and last time that I'd ever have plenty of money to spend on the music!

---

[3] One of a series of programmes on communication. The generic series title never reached the catalogue.

Faced with such riches, I hired a sizeable number of musicians and set my sights high. This was to be a score of stellar proportions.

Pride comes before a fall, and my enthusiasm far outstripped my skill. I was not experienced in orchestration, and even less so in running a session with so many players. So green about conducting, I hadn't even grasped the fact that musicians follow the conductor's beat; to the casual observer they are lagging some way behind. I became so concerned with this that I started conducting to their beat, which meant they dutifully followed that. The tempo slowed. It was clear I was not cut out for this.

So, there I was at the top of the stairs, unhappy with the results of the live session, when an obvious thought struck me. Why was I using old orchestral sounds anyway, after all this was a programme about something new? Even if the session had gone to plan, the result would have been familiar stuff, and not as groundbreaking as the subject of the programme.

It was about 6 o'clock in the evening. The director of the broadcast would be eager to hear how the session had gone, and I knew that something had to be pulled out of the hat.

Paddy, Roger and I had been sharing the ARP Odyssey synthesiser. It was one of the most creative pieces of gear I've ever come across. You would stumble across an interesting sound by experimenting, and then have to decipher how it had happened. It forced you to learn. Of course, in those days nothing was memorised, and so you had to be sure you could reprogram it later.

I started to play around on the ARP. There are one or two automated features on it, including a repeated note trigger. I played a low E. The note repeated over and over but was too bright. Turning down the filter I noticed that you could also trigger the opening and closing of the filter with the same note repeater. Things started to sound interesting, but mechanical.

We'd all inherited the techniques that had gone before in the Workshop, and none more so than the amazing things you could do with tape manipulation. The quarter inch tape recorders formed an invaluable part of the creative gear in the studio. If you set them to run at seven and a half inches a second, they gave a useful echo effect, but the wrong speed for the repeating E. It was easier to change the original notes on the synthesiser than change the tape, so I lowered the LFO (Low Frequency Oscillator) which was controlling their speed, and something rather unexpected happened. There was one point at which the rhythm accelerated into a gallop. The first note was now being echoed after the second note had sounded, which was being echoed after the third, and so on. The simplest phrase suddenly became intricate. This was the turning point in the writing of what was to become one of my best known tracks, 'The Astronauts'.

There has to be that moment in any successful electronic piece when the sound itself becomes the source of the ideas. It can be anything[4]. There has to be a trigger, a catalyst, without which the rest wouldn't exist. You need to take a leap in the dark. My lack of knowledge about a lot of this gear meant I'd try things with little knowledge of the outcome. That was what was missing from my session music. I'd mistakenly thought a big budget would improve the music. I realise now, after all these years, that it's time spent becoming familiar with a piece of equipment that will reward you with ideas. It's real team work.

I worked throughout that night, and came up with what we now recognise as the bass trundle sound of 'The Astronauts', together with the basic theme. I played the result to the director, who was thankfully delighted. I omitted to mention that this was not the result of that expensive session he had paid for, and he omitted to ask. After all, he had got what he wanted and felt it was money well spent.

---

[4] A recent piece hinges on a discovery made in the deep recesses of Reaktor.

Sometimes our failures represent a path we need to travel to get to our destination, I think I read that on a wall somewhere; probably on the underground.

Anyway by the beginning of June 1975, my work on *Space for Man* was finished, and the music filed away. I got on with other projects.

Two years later in 1977, whilst putting together a solo album for BBC Records[5], the music for *Space for Man* would get another airing. Side One of the album was a magnum opus called 'In the Kingdom of Colours', but Side Two a selection of individual tracks. I'd just finished working on a **Horizon** special called *The Case Of The Ancient Astronauts*[6]. The music was suitably grand and featured a long two minute opening. It started with a sequenced run on the Synthi 100, followed by a mixture of tape manipulation and synthesiser lines to depict the footsteps of the ancient astronauts. Making album music from programme music can sometimes be tricky and this piece needed a good end sequence. If possible, something that already existed. 'Space for Man' seemed an obvious choice, and was even in the same key, E minor.

It was only at this stage that the music was enlarged to contain some of the memorable sections that audiences now expect; the middle 8 and the section with the timpani drums.

I was using a rear internal studio at that time, deep under the apex of BBC Maida Vale. Next to it was an acoustic studio, accessible via a small corridor, which led off the long main corridor of the building.

We all had a good relationship with the players of the BBC Symphony Orchestra and used the services of soloists frequently. There were so few bars of timpani to play, that I persuaded one of the orchestral

---

[5] *Through A Glass Darkly*. We'll come back to this later in the book.
[6] In fact, the entry date for 'Ancient Astronauts' and for *Through a Glass Darkly* is precisely the same, 1/8/1977, but the album had been under preparation for many months.

percussionists to arrange for the drums to be brought up during his lunch hour. They didn't even get as far as the studio and were deposited in the small corridor. Rather than wheel them any further, we just recorded them where they stood, and in half an hour it was all done.

So, the newly enlarged and polished 'Space for Man' was attached to the recently finished 'Ancient Astronauts' and the last track on Side Two of the solo album was complete.

Three years later, having risked an entire career[7] in remaking the **Doctor Who** title music, we were looking for something suitable for the B side of the single release[8]. Two tracks from the solo album were considered, 'Magenta Court' and 'The Astronauts', and of course 'The Astronauts' won.

There I was, hiding on the flip side, hanging on the coat tails of the **Doctor Who** theme[9]. It was going to be a wonderful opportunity if anyone bothered to listen. I shared a flat once with a girl who never ever played B sides, not even of LPs. She assumed that anything labelled B was not as good as A, and in this case she would have been right. Still, I lived in hope.

I've received many wonderful letters and emails from people about 'The Astronauts'. One emailer talks about him playing it repeatedly every night until his parents could stand it no more. Another about how it was part of the sounds of his growing up. Well, it was part of my growing up too. Perhaps it was the first time at the Workshop that I realised, changing your mind, changing everything on a whim, is not always such a bad idea. That decision at the top of the stairs really paid off.

Throwing everything in the air and starting again is a good way to solve problems. I've never been weighed down by any strict expectations and

---

[7] Well, perhaps not an entire career, but I certainly felt as if I was treading on egg shells.
[8] A single of 'The Astronauts' had earlier been released alongside the album.
[9] If not coat tails, then at least a very long scarf.

have never perfected playing or performing music. Every project for me is a bit like starting again. The wheels on this bus seem to come off at the end of every trip, and it makes progress slow at times. The lack of accruing expertise leads to a relentless need to make it better and because I've never passed any sort of music exam or played well in any conventional sense, this can take it in unexpected directions. What started out bad, can end up different.

I've had tinnitus, a high pitched constant squeak in the ears, from an early age. I used to detune a radio off station and listen to the resulting white noise quietly in the background, in order to go to sleep at night. Sounding like the sea in the distance, it would mask the noise in my head by taking the sound into the space around me. This might explain why I ended up in sound design and composition.

Of course, it's not all spontaneous reaction. A lot of stuff has found its way under the hood over the years, but it has a lot more to do with the craft and skill of the job rather than the actual act of composing. The way pictures suggest and help you write the music greatly enhances your ability to do the job, but deep down it's that same creativity in the driving seat, and that never really changes however much you improve the craft. However you look at it, there's a lot of hard graft involved. Nothing new is cheap.

Working Out

The Workshop contained a number of composers, all of whom will have different stories to tell about how and why they ended up writing music for Television and Radio. There were nine people entered in the catalogue as composers in 1976 and the department handled a total of 283 projects.

Dick Mills lead the field with 63 jobs to his name. Supplying sounds rather than music, the projects were shorter and faster, and he would clock up many more titles. On the other hand, whole series were often a single entry in the catalogue, so it hard to be precise.

It's easy to imagine that work was a neat sequential line of projects but it was more chaotic. However linear the commissioning of the music, different programmes would jostle for priority. You'd have to work on several projects at once in order to meet the deadlines.

Here's a list of all my work during 1976 taken from the Radiophonic Catalogue...

The Dark Labyrinth	January 1976		Radio 4
Finger on the Pulse	January 1976	Current Affairs	Radio 4
Spells for Schools	January 1976	Features, Art & Education	Radio 4 Schools
Music Club: Hen Pizzicato	January 1976		Radio 4
World About Us: Cree Indians	January 1976	Features	BBC2
Ear Slapping	February 1976	Edinburgh	Regional Radio
Glyndebourne - An Opera in Production	February 1976	Creative Radio	Radio 3
Daedalus Equations (Mind Beyond)	March 1976	Drama	Television Music & Sounds
Hermit's Island	March 1976	Music	Radio 3

A Question of Ulster	March 1976	Current Affairs	Television
Radio Ulster Jingles	March 1976	Radio Ulster	Jingles
Sound by Design	April 1976	Continuing Education	Radio 3
A Country of Nations	April 1976	Current Affairs	BBC1
Festival 40	June 1976	TV Presentation	Television
The Cavemen Cometh	June 1976	Drama	Radio
Games and Puzzles	July 1976	Bristol	Radio
A Man for all Theatres	July 1976	Drama	Radio 4
Sinatra in Hollywood	July 1976	TV Presentation	Television
West Cumbria at One	August 1976	Radio Carlisle	Local Radio
M101 (Maths) Titles	August 1976	Open University	Television
The Secret War	August 1976	TV Science Features	Television
City Limits	September 1976	Radio Manchester	Radio
James and the Giant Peach	October 1976	Childrens	Television
You and Yours Signature Tune	December 1976	Current Affairs	Radio 4
OU Maths Signature Tune	December 1976	Open University	Radio

| M101 (short Version) | December 1976 | Open University | Television |

A whole collection of radio projects threaded in out of the work for television. There were eighteen projects for radio, idents for a local radio station, title tunes, complete radio dramas and a radio documentary. Outside composers were always envious of us in the Radiophonic Workshop, where work never stopped, but we often longed for a bit of head space. The BBC's need for music seemed unstoppable.

A short piece was needed for the Swahili section of BBC World Service. I wasn't keen. It brought back some embarrassing memories.

Like every studio manager, I was seconded there shortly after the initial training in the Langham. I needed to answer two questions. Would I like to work for the World Service, and would the World Service like me to? I didn't, and they didn't.

My heart wasn't in it, and I kept making mistakes. The worst one was for the Swahili service.

The studio managers at Bush House had to make the announcements between the programmes. This was achieved via a microphone in the control room on the mixing desk, so that you could make the announcement whilst mixing the programme. In order to stop unpleasant ringing feedback when you turned on the mic, all the output in the control room was silenced when the mic was on. Several of my colleagues had left the mic on by mistake, so it was a known issue, but that didn't stop me doing the same thing.

Night shifts were common at Bush House, since they were broadcasting to different time zones around the world, and I was tired. I made the announcement and then faded up the opening music of the programme.

Silence.

Panic set in.

It so happens that I was not alone in the control room. The head of the Swahili section had come down to see the programme broadcast. He and I started a conversation about what might have gone wrong, lasting a minute or so. Suddenly, I realised that the mic switch was still on and as soon as I switched it off, the music came on and the programme continued.

Embarrassingly the listeners to that Swahili broadcast would have heard our entire conversation.

"Is the tape playing?"

"Yes, it seems to be."

"I just can't understand it, it was working just now when I tested it."

There's one redeeming fact about this whole sorry tale. During the night at Bush House the staff is very sparse, and I'm pleased to say that the only person in the UK who would have been the slightest bit concerned about this serious error, was sitting beside me contributing to it.

The Swahili music passed off without incident and the next project slid under the door.

This was in every sense a production line and one which was still equipped with a rather sparse set of gear. We had two VCS3s, the Synthi 100, ARP Odyssey and Yamaha SY2.

A lot of commentators have assumed that the new synths had taken over our world, but old ways remained. In part, because there were still many things that we couldn't do without resorting to old techniques[10]. In 1976, in the same room as the ARP synth, I'd laboriously repitched chicken clucks to make them sing the Pizzicato[11] from Léo Delibes' 'Sylvia'. The new batch of synths could not effectively manipulate audio, and yet that was at the very core of the Workshop's output. In any case, we were all in awe of the music and sound that the Workshop had already produced, and keen to learn how to use those techniques in our own music.

It would take nine years for that situation to change, twenty-two years after the arrival of the new synthesisers in 1963.

Harder Times

We were regarded with great suspicion by the Musicians' Union in the late seventies. They accused the department of cheapening music by the use of modern shortcuts, and of being completely without talent. Of course we had talent, but not as much as them. In their eyes we were stealing work from their members, which was factually correct, but not as big an issue as they were making out. Our operation was tiny. The BBC produced many specially composed pieces every year, but the Workshop contributed only a small fraction of them. Of those, many were for the cash-strapped BBC Schools department, who could not afford to use musicians anyway. The Musicians' Union were still unhappy, and during a strike around that time, our workplace was only accessible through a picket line.

The irony was that we had very good relations with musicians and have continued to have ever since[12]. They were always only too pleased to play for us.

---

[10] This would be repeated during our next major upheaval, the advent of digital.
[11] In the catalogue as 'Hen Pizzicato'.
[12] No more proof is needed than the welcome Mark Ayres and I got when we joined the Welsh Symphony Orchestra for the Doctor Who Prom in 2013.

But the mood remained tricky. Made even trickier when a TV presenter referred to the Radiophonic Workshop as…

"The place you go to get the sound of a full orchestra from a box."

So, given the tension, I was surprised when a friend asked me if she and her partner, a classical lute player, might come and visit my studio.

On their arrival I was immediately struck by their sense of adventure; they were entering a forbidden realm.

Composer	Peter Howell	TRW No.8446
Title	Games and Puzzles	
Series		
Producer	Moira Mann	
Department	Bristol	
Requirement Service	Radio	
Company Notes	Excerpts also on PH-DAT	

I was working on a very short piece called 'Games and Puzzles'[13], achieved entirely on the ARP synthesiser. I played it to them, which to the lute player must have sounded like tinnitus. In order to fill the silence that followed, and to distract us from the tumbleweed which blew through the studio, I reached for the ARP keyboard.

"This is how I got the main sound," I said.

I started to play the synthesiser through the mixer and out of the speakers.

The lute player visibly jumped.

---

[13] I really hope that was a working title.

"My God. The sound's coming out over there."

It had never occurred to me, but to those classical players who have never ventured outside their tightly sealed world, an instrument that could throw its voice was the work of the devil.

Here was a performer who spent a lot of his time playing the music of long-deceased composers, trying to find some common ground in the lair of one who was still alive. It was a hard ask[14]. Experiment and improvisation come naturally to someone like me with such a wayward musical technique. A far cry from the composer in the garret pouring over a score.

There have been many occasions when I've composed a piece without knowing (or to be honest caring) what key it was in, how the beats divided up into bars, whether the parts were playable, or even whether it was a coherent piece of music.

The lute player was already planning his escape.

The Daedulus Equations[15] was to be my first taste of working with television drama. The film told the story of Hans Daedulus who defected from East to West Germany, and how his mathematical work lived on. As was often the case in those days, we would provide special sound as well as music. My task was to cover those sequences in the film which dealt with the maths equations themselves as if they were disembodied entities and separate from the main thrust of the narrative.

Working for TV was very much more time consuming than radio, because everything you did had to be synchronised[16]. TV projects would take up most your time.

---

[14] I might be exaggerating his cautiousness to anything Radiophonic because I managed to persuade him to play lute on the **Doctor Who** adventure, *The King's Demons*.
[15] *The Mind Beyond: The Daedalus Equations*, **BBC2 Playhouse**, 20 October 1976.
[16] The music had to match the pictures, frame for frame.

They all started with a meeting. In radio, with the producer, and in television the director. In the BBC this meeting tended to be called a 'Briefing' but the industry generally referred to it as a 'Spotting Session'. I got to rely on these meetings. Psycho-analysing the director led to better results.

By looking them in the eyes, you could work out why they were asking for the music. Was it to cover up mistakes on their part, or was it really there to advance the narrative?

Whatever the reason, I always tried to be positive about the film. The director will have been nursing this particular baby for many months and was understandably nervous about it.

I tried to come away from each of these meetings with a good idea of what was required. A few successful projects convinced me that the system was working and my probation period was coming to an end; but I was wrong. Too many things had been for granted, and the next thing to come through the door would smash my confidence to bits.

The Rookie and the Professional

Anna Home, who later was to be one of the founding producers of **EastEnders**, rang Desmond Briscoe to ask for a composer to work on a television adaptation of Roald Dahl's *James and the Giant Peach*.

The brief included songs and instrumental underscore for the action. I'd long been hinting to Desmond that I'd written many songs before joining the Workshop and felt ready to tackle something like this.

After a short time, I met Paul Stone, the director. We settled on a list of songs and where in the story they would occur, and I left the meeting having agreed to produce them in demo form[17]. The assignment felt like a perfect match for me, and I couldn't wait to get started.

After two weeks, I sent the demos off and with one exception, all the songs were approved.

Desmond Briscoe had agreed with the producer that as well as composing the songs, I would also attend rehearsals to teach the actors to sing them. I'd co-produced five shows full of songs in Sussex prior to joining the BBC, and was looking forward it.

The BBC owned a tower block in Acton in those days. Basically each floor was divided into two large spaces, which could be allocated to any production. So, at any one time the building would be full of different groups of people rehearsing all sorts of shows. As you can imagine, the canteen in Acton Rehearsal Rooms was like a *Who's Who* of actors, singers, and dancers.

On the way up to the second floor on the first day, I shared the lift with Bruce Forsyth, who at that time was doing a regular variety show. I was struck by his height, which was less than expected and his energy and fitness, which was a great deal more. He got out at the first floor, and I continued up to the second.

All the cast were there, Pat Coombs, Hugh Lloyd, Thorley Walters[18], and Bernard Cribbins. After a few brief introductions, I started teaching Bernard one of my songs. What he, and they, expected and what I could deliver were two very different things. It was that sudden, and it came as a shock on many levels. This wasn't amateur night in a Sussex village hall, this was professional, these were professionals, every one of them with

---

[17] A demo is a piece of music or a song that gives an impression of the final piece. It will usually have a stand-in voice, and rough instrumental sounds that will be replaced by session musicians if the idea is accepted.
[18] The most celebrated and experienced member of the cast, here appearing in one of his last roles.

more experience than I would garner in my entire career.

Worse still, not only was I lacking experience, but I was also lacking skill. They had assumed that just because I was a composer I was also naturally able to act as a rehearsal pianist.

Rehearsal pianists have many talents, but I suppose the one thing they possess that I and a lot of composers lack, is the ability to repitch what they are reading and playing in any key in real time. One of the first things a singer will want to ensure, even before they start to rehearse a song, is that the range of notes they are asked to sing, comes easily to their singing voice without strain. It became clear that I was unable to instantly change the key of the accompaniment to suit the singers. In short, I was a composer, not a rehearsal pianist. The director of the show had made some assumptions[19] when I was hired, and now two things had happened. I was made to feel about two inches tall, and worse still, any confidence the cast might have had in my ability to pull this off was shattered. This was not a good day at the office.

The craziest thing, looking back, was that all the songs had been accepted by everyone, including the actors. I'd stupidly thought that it was all that was required of me. The BBC was, and is, a broadcasting stage that allows performers from all sections of the entertainment world to do what they do. They expect to be able to function as much as possible in the way that they function in their own sphere of work, working with people who have experience and maturity and can be relied upon.

I muddled through as best I could, but the whole saga was a terrible setback for me. I'd only been at the Workshop two years, but it felt long enough to be able to pull off writing a few songs. It would be about four years before I felt as if I could do the job properly.

---

[19] Years later, John Nathan-Turner made the assumption that I could act as Musical Director in a pantomime he was producing. On that occasion, I was sensible enough to tell him that it was just not my thing!

A long time after this debacle, I went to see *Guys and Dolls* at the National Theatre. Bernard Cribbins was playing Nathan Detroit.

It was a great revival of a stunning musical, but in this performance there was a technical problem in the second act. Some scenery got stuck during the change from one scene to another. There was a noticeable pause whist everyone tried to work out what to do. We in the audience were left waiting for something to happen. Bernard Cribbins was on stage at the time, and he looked towards the audience, and moved down to the footlights, whilst slowly removing his hat. He was no longer in character, we all realised this, the hat had gone, and so had Nathan Detroit. This was Bernard Cribbins. He had the audience in the palm of his hand, regaling them with jokes and anecdotes. After what must have been over five minutes, it was clear that the technical problem had been fixed, the scenery moved into position and Bernard Cribbins quietly walked back into his position in the new set and put on the hat. Nathan Detroit was in the room again, and the show continued.

I thought back to the rehearsals for *James and the Giant Peach*. There had been a rookie and a professional in that room, and no doubt about which was which.

Stockholm

Is this really it?

We are playing in Stockholm tonight.

The Transit van full of gear has travelled through northern Europe (France, Holland, Germany, Denmark, and across the bridge to Sweden). We've used a plane.

Sometime, I must come back to Stockholm to find out what it's really like, because none of our experiences on this trip seem to match up to what I'd been told. The guy driving us from the airport tells us repeatedly that he is about to move to the States, our hotel's in a part of Stockholm that resembles Hove on a wet Sunday afternoon, and the venue we are playing reminds me of the Hackney Empire.

Where's the cold crisp windswept waterfront? The saunas and the pine? Come to that, where's Wallander?

Dick Mills and I make a trip to the centre of Stockholm to try to persuade ourselves it's all there somewhere. We don't quite make it all the way and stop at a coffee shop. We've both noticed something rather odd. As you walk down the small pedestrianised streets, there's hardly any chatter. Even on the narrow paths between the high buildings, you hear no voices. Now this could be for one of two reasons; they are all frightened of being overheard, fearing some sort of surveillance, or—and I think this is more likely—they are content. They have no reason to raise their voices; all's well. I need to go back to see if I'm right.

Our venue's a large old theatre, in which an entire festival is taking place: the Red Bull Music Academy Weekender. It's strange to think a drink that tastes of (what is that exactly?) has acquired enough clout to have its own festival. There are several performance areas in this one building. Sound from one part of the building finds its way to another. Our front of house PA system is often on the high side, with plenty of bass—for a group of people who spent all their working lives writing music for speakers in the side of TVs, it's understandable. So, in the event, we hear very little of the other stages; it's us who interfere with them.

When playing abroad, it's always hard to gauge how much your audience will recognise things, and some advance research has to be done. In the event, they're an appreciative crowd and the concert seems to have gone well. After de-rigging the big value items such as computers, we find our way back to the dressing room. This is a space on a different floor, positioned between two different parts of the building; it's got a door at both ends. This most definitely used to be a corridor. We are just getting to grips with the Swedish beers and other goodies in the fridge, when the alarm goes off. It's clear after a minute or two that we all need to evacuate the building, and so grabbing the valuables, we exit down the stairs, holding our glasses of beer.

Outside, we have to gather opposite the front of the building. There isn't much light and a lot of people are crammed into a tight space but everyone's in good spirits, despite having their night curtailed.

It's a few minutes before I realise I've left my laptop in the dressing room, but I have my glass of beer so that's all right. I stand there allowing the full import of what has happened to sink in. The other members of the band, although sympathetic, want to get back to the hotel and I agree to see them there, once I've retrieved my belongings. I try to persuade one of the stewards to let me back in. He refuses, at least I think he does[1]. Eventually, I resign myself to just standing there and waiting. At this moment, a couple appear at my side. One of them's keen to get my autograph and as I'm signing, I explain my predicament. Their solution is to go and have a drink with them to pass the time. I agree and we find our way to a bar alongside the building which is thronging with people. It's almost as if it had been set up especially to cater for people evacuated from the building. Perhaps this business' success relies entirely on the faulty fire alarm next door. After a quarter of an hour or so, the festival manager appears as if out of nowhere. How does he know I'm here?

He volunteers to go back into the building to retrieve my laptop. I should be more grateful, but I'm intrigued by these new friends.

The couple turn out to be Swedish and Italian, and they seem to enjoy travelling back and forth to each of those countries catching whatever gig interests them.

Do they ever work? It seems a stupid question.

Whenever I speak to people who attend our concerts, I'm always struck by how they can release themselves completely from their everyday selves and just be there in the moment, enjoying it all for what it is. We are in the escapism business and always have been, even in the old days working out of a studio.

---

[1] I've consumed all the Scandi thrillers, and I still don't speak Swedish.

Keeping Pace

I still have fond memories of those technical bits and pieces in the pre-digital era. It was so hands on. The word 'virtual' still meant 'almost but not quite', and the studio was so full of stuff, it looked like the set of **Steptoe and Son**. You'd wander round the room looking for the right sound. Tinkling glasses, playing with combs, hitting things, like an old 35mm film can lid in the corner of the room. That one proved ideal for 'The Case of the Ancient Astronauts', the **Horizon** Special I mentioned earlier, about the wild claims of Erich von Däniken[2].

As ever, before work started, a 'Spotting Session' would take place. The meeting with the director to discuss the proposed music.

I always asked an initial question that affected everything that followed. *"Is the film for BBC1 or BBC2?"*

In other words, is this a red top tabloid or a broadsheet?

Remember, around this time the BBC only had two networks. BBC1 for everyday material and BBC2 for more thoughtful stuff; in many ways it resembled BBC4 today[3].

Sometimes at these sessions, it became clear that the director was expecting an unreasonable amount of music from you. I always tried to have a 'can do' approach, but sometimes expectations were just too high. You had to ask yourself, "If I was to stay awake from this moment until the final mix, would I finish the work?"

There really were many occasions when the answer would have been 'no'. Deadlines were always tight, but they had to be achievable.

---

[2] This unusual scientist had suggested that ancient astronauts had visited the Earth a long time ago, and had drawn strange lines in a Mexican desert, as well as building the Egyptian pyramids. I think sliced bread might have been one of theirs, too.

[3] BBC4 might well be a casualty in the latest cost cutting round.

So, I might suggest delivering the material in batches; the most important cues first, followed by filler material, and then just mop up with very simple extras at the end. That way the first burst of work would involve the most creative input.

There were around thirty cues in 'The Case of the Ancient Astronauts', including opening and closing music. It was going to be a tense fortnight, made worse by some over indulgence. The opening sequence of this programme took far too long, which meant subsequent cues were tight for time.

Language Programme (Pilot)	May 1977	SP05 Education	Radio Scotland Schools
Mechanical Voices	May 1977	SP05 Education	Radio Scotland Schools
Fanfare	May 1977	Music	Radio 3
Radio Wales News Jingles	July 1977	Radio Wales	Radio Wales
The Case of the Ancient Astronauts	July 1977	TV Science Features	BBC2 Horizon
The Tale of the Knight, the Witch & the Dragon	August 1977	Drama	Radio 4 Drama

Next out of the pipe was a radio drama of no great consequence.

There were many memorable productions from BBC Radio's drama department. *The Tale of the Knight, the Witch & the Dragon* was not one of them. The title said it all, there was nothing more to add.

The knight, in this run-of-the-mill radio drama, was played by Patrick Stewart, long before he commanded the Enterprise as Jean-Luc Picard. I can't remember who played the witch, but I played the dragon. In order to make an otherwise interminable day go with a swing, the director decided to feature the dragon live in the studio. So, I sat around with the actors during the read through, making a roaring sound through a cardboard tube. The centre of a kitchen roll, to be precise. My heart wasn't in it.

I'd agreed to write music and produce some special sounds for this radio production, but I expected the sounds to be made back in my studio. When the director invited me to the recording, I assumed it was out of courtesy, but it was clearly out of need. He was one Studio Manager down, and I ended doing the spot effects[4] throughout the day.

I only mention it here because of the horses. There were a lot of them in this script, in fact the characters in this drama were rarely off them.

To make it sound more immediate, the horses hooves would be played off effects disc in the control room, but the harness sound was to come from the studio. We fiddled around for a while, trying to find the right sound and eventually came up with house keys. All the actors had some in their pocket. For some reason Patrick Stewart found holding his script and jangling his keys hard, because he needed to turn the pages every now and then. I was volunteered to shake them in time with his 'riding'. He was taking this seriously and suggested that to get his voice to sound as if he was on horseback, he would bend his knees and bob up and down. I would then have to match my key jangling to his knee bends. I was somewhat in awe of this guy, he was already well known as a Shakespearean actor, and I would have liked to have had a serious conversation with him, but that was out of the question. He clearly wouldn't be interested in talking to his horse.

---

[4] Sounds made live in the studio with the actors.

The music and the final production came and went. Nobody asked for their licence fee back. It was a success.

All the composers at the time had been Studio Managers in Broadcasting House, so they arrived with studio skills. This was to come in very handy when we were volunteered[5] for Desmond Briscoe's special radio features. He produced these entirely at the Workshop, and so we were responsible for delivering a final broadcast master. In our day to day work this was rarely the case, because we delivered inserts that were mixed into the master elsewhere.

I felt that I was seconded to these features more often than most, but it gave me an insight into how they were developed, and the deadlines and pressures involved.

Working for Desmond was always an experience. His meticulousness one day and complete disengagement the next, led to some memorable moments.

The fifty minute Radio 3 documentary *A Wall Walks Slowly*[6] was littered with short remarks from a whole host of characters. Desmond insisted on the precise panning of each voice in the stereo image, a position that they would occupy whenever they spoke. With no automation, this was a challenge, one which, at some points in the programme, completely defeated me. Seeing my desperation, the Workshop engineers came to the rescue with a voltage-controlled panning device, without which I'd have been taken away by men in white coats.

Then, at the other end of the scale, I found myself working twenty-seven hours non stop to meet a deadline, with Desmond asleep in the corner of the studio for the last seven. He then asked me to drive the resulting master tape to Broadcasting House in time for its broadcast. They were

---

[5] Is that the right word? He was the boss, so it was hard to say 'no'.
[6] I also composed the music for this feature which was set in Cumbria and featured the poems of Norman Nicholson. The programme won the Sony Gold Award in 1977.

good programmes and were well received, but my appreciation of them was rather dimmed by exhaustion.

Although these one off specials were regular, they were not frequent. We had no budget of our own and relied on goodwill from above; our managers and their managers would not look kindly on a department spending too much time on vanity projects[7]. There was always this draw back to our core function as a facility for programme makers across the BBC. It stopped us getting too big for our boots.

A Wall Walks Slowly, like many other projects, featured recorded musicians as well as the radiophonic content, and my lack of classical musical education has always made writing scores for these sessions[8] hard. For someone who grew up in a home studio, memorising songs and instrumentals just long enough to record them, the thought of having to describe music in advance so that someone else can play it, can be odd and unnerving.

Over the years, I've become accustomed to the process, but back in my early days at the Workshop, I was sailing very close to the wind whenever I hired session players. My knowledge of scoring was acquired on the job, and at a time when there was no computer assistance.

Right from the start I came across what looked like intractable problems. The strange world of transposition, where a player would see a note 'C' and play a note 'C' and deliver another pitch altogether, was utterly uncalled for. Rather like medieval priests choosing to conduct all liturgical conversations in Latin, it seemed to be designed to keep ordinary people from ever joining in. This wilful distortion of reality required the player's score to be written down in a different key to the key of the music itself. Pure Lewis Carroll[9].

---

[7] Despite this we managed to slip a few into the schedules.
[8] A studio recording of live musicians.
[9] "Is that the name of the song?" asked Alice. "No" said the White Knight. "That's just what it's called." (abridged)

Luckily, after a while I realised that contrary to my initial fears, musicians did have my best interests at heart. They would willingly come to my aid if it turned out that I'd transposed in the wrong direction, giving them an unplayable score, or had completely forgotten to transpose at all.

I ought to stress that I did make a concerted effort to improve my musical skills, but every time I tried, the same thing would happen. I would gain a small improvement in my abilities in sight reading or score writing, and sacrifice everything that allowed me to write the music in the first place. My intuitive self seemed to be completely submerged in a set of rules created by somebody else. There's an old and much quoted Irish saying that sums it up perfectly.

"If you want to go there, I wouldn't start from here."

I had come too far down one path. To take another one, required backtracking a long way to the fork in the road, and choosing the other way. My attempts at doing just that have resulted in a passable knowledge of score writing that has allowed me to communicate with musicians, and that's something that has been invaluable, but any attempt to go further up that road seems to shut off my creative supply.

There are clearly those who have discovered a third and middle way, and are able to write creatively without compromising their strict musical upbringing, and I have taught many of them at the NFTS[10]. They are more plentiful, I think, because music and technology are now so intertwined that they can see the bigger picture from the start of their education.

With my conventional musical skill being so limited, I've grown to appreciate just how clever these session musicians really are. The high fees they can command for a three hour recording session are worth every penny. You're tapping into a vast pool of skill and if you feel that

---

[10] The National Film and Television School.

you have paid too much, then perhaps it's your score or lack of direction that haven't used their talent to the full.

The Radiophonic Workshop had always used professional musicians to add to otherwise electronic scores, and with the proximity of the BBC Symphony Orchestra offices just up the corridor, it became easier to book and use many of their players. Perhaps the word 'many' gives the wrong impression. Over the years we did use many, but generally only one or two at a time. The cost of the players was above the line, whereas the Workshop fell below the line, so programme budgets wouldn't allow large ensembles.

Nevertheless, the use of just one live instrument against radiophonic content could have a dramatic effect. For example, I provided the score for a series on the human brain. The content seems so old fashioned today but at the time it brought us up to date with contemporary research. I decided to represent the circuitry of the brain with electronic music and human consciousness with the rich sound of a viola.

Over the many years of the Radiophonic Workshop, the composers have dealt with many subjects in documentaries, and over that time have absorbed a small amount from each. Certain sequences stay with you, and this one really resonates with the way that any of us so-called creatives get through the day.

There's a scene in **The Human Brain** where a woman is choosing clothes to wear for a night out.

She goes to the wardrobe, picks a top and skirt, returns to the bed where she lays them on the bedspread to decide whether she has made the right choice. But instead, without pausing, she returns to the wardrobe and selects two more items. This sequence repeats itself over and over until all the clothes from the wardrobe are on the bed, and no choice had been made. The left side of her brain, responsible for the organising, is dealing with the fetching and carrying, and the right side is dealing with the aesthetic decisions about colour and suitability, and is in charge of her preferences. Both sides are working normally, but because she has suffered from an extreme form of epilepsy and has had the bridge between the halves of her brain removed, the left side never gets the message that the right side has made a choice, and so continues to fetch more clothes.

Interesting, perhaps, but why mention this here?

Because the whole left brain / right brain thing seems to be of enormous importance to those of us that try to make something creative out of something technical. Our right brains would be lost without the methodical left brain having read the manual and figured out how the gear worked. I'm glad to say my bridge is still intact.

My First Brush with the Doctor

Although famous for Delia's rendition of the **Doctor Who** title music, the Workshop was only peripherally involved in the incidental music. Deadlines were tight, and the time taken to produce anything of quality was long. It would be impossible for us to complete the necessary amount of music in time for each broadcast.

Right from the early days, incidental music for **Doctor Who** had been composed, arranged and conducted by Dudley Simpson[11], an Australian musician and composer who established a quite idiosyncratic way of meeting those deadlines.

He used our services to add electronic lines to his otherwise more conventional music, and I was lucky enough to be involved in one of his scores.

---

[11] Sadly, Dudley passed away in 2017.

I was invited to the session recording of the live musicians at BBC Lime Grove. These studios had previously been used to shoot feature films including *20,000 Leagues Under the Sea*. In fact, in order to get to the music recording studio, I passed the massive tank that was used for many of the closeup water sequences. Going to Lime Grove was always somewhat of an adventure. On another occasion, peering through the small window in the door of Studio 1, I just managed to spot Ronnie Barker and Ronnie Corbett running through a number. They were marching on the spot in the middle of a large group of brass players[12]. The song has since appeared in all the 'Best of...' compilations.

When I arrived at the recording studio, the musicians were already set up and ready to go, with Leslie Pearson sitting at a large organ-like keyboard, and the percussionist Tristram Fry standing in front of an array of percussion: marimba, cymbals, drums, bell tree, and large orchestral timpani. As the session progressed, he would athletically dash up and down this corridor of instruments, doing the work of several musicians and earning his 'doubling fee'[13] several times over.

I positioned myself in the control room by the recording equipment, and made sure I had a good view of the musicians in the studio through the glass. Before the session started, Dudley came into the room brandishing a 7 inch tape box, and walked up to the tape operator.

"*I need you to run this constantly on this machine,*" he said, brandishing it. "*Then feed the output through to my headphones in the studio.*"

Clearly, the operator had never done this sort of thing before.

"*It's 15 inches long. It's got a blip of tone on it,*" he added by way of

---

[12] 'The Aldershot Brass Ensemble', a sketch from the 26 December, 1977 edition of **The Two Ronnies**.
[13] An artist would get paid more for playing more than one instrument. In this case, normal percussion such as drums and cymbals, tuned percussion such as marimba, and timpani drums.

explanation, omitting to mention that it was in fact a tape loop, a ring of tape.

The tape machines ran at 15 inches per second in those days, and this loop would feed a blip to Dudley in the studio every second. It was a such a great idea, it deserves to be explained, even though doing so might cause you to glaze over!

When I looked at Dudley's scores for the session, the tempo of every cue of music was either 60 bpm[14], 120 bpm or compounds thereof. To ensure the recording synced with the action in the shots, there had to be a clear correlation between the tempo of the music and the passing seconds. Many people used some quite mind bogglingly complex calculations to predict what various tempos would deliver, but Dudley had by-passed all that. He had a reliable technique. If there was a constant blip in his ear every second, and every tempo was 60 bpm or multiples of that, he could predict how the music would fit the picture without any time consuming maths. Of course, the only drawback was the limited number of tempos that he could work with. But even with that constraint, he could still deliver tightly synchronised music for any scene. He would give the musicians strange sub divisions in the bars, that could hit any of the cue points on screen. By using a small group of skilled players, he succeeded in shifting the complexity caused by varying tempos onto the score itself. Genius.

All the way through the process, from writing, the session recording, to the addition of the electronics, Dudley had perfected an efficient labour saving method of ensuring the deadlines were met.

Once the session was complete, the multitrack tapes were shipped up to Maida Vale and loaded onto the Studer machine in Radiophonic Studio A, alongside the massive Synthi 100 synthesiser. It was my job to tease some decent sounds out of the synthesiser, that Dudley would then play,

---

[14] Beats per Minute. So 60 bpm is a beat per second.

adding electronics to the session recordings. In addition, towards the end of the day, we would record a mix of all these multi tracks onto quarter inch tape, which would be shipped back to Television Centre for the final mix. Having done that, the multitrack tapes were of no further use to the production, and were stored in the cupboards under the Synthi 100[15].

Dudley had another trick up his sleeve.

One of the abiding challenges was to try to match the music with the epic scale of the stories, using only small forces of musicians and a monophonic synthesiser. Composers at the Workshop got round this restriction by doing multiple passes, and recording every successive voice in a harmony on each pass, but that was a long process, and Dudley would simply not have had the time. Of course, he had a way round it.

He would write large chords for the synthesiser, but they would rigidly travel up and down the keyboard in the same configuration. Imagine super-glueing your fingers to spread out and play a complex chord, and then simply move up the keyboard without altering the spread. You could pitch the many oscillators to all the different pitches of the big chord, creating a really big sound, and then play them all at once with a single note. So, an epic sound could be achieved just by playing a solo line. One limitation would be that the harmonies would sound a little strange at times, but then the whole arrangement of the music was written with that in mind. Providing it was not overused, it added much needed scale to an otherwise thinner score.

Dudley's pragmatic approach delivered the best possible result given the time and the technology; but once we were responsible for the whole score, there was always an expectation that the Radiophonic Workshop would deliver something special, despite the time available. Sometimes, you didn't need reminding of just how tight these deadlines were. You'd

---

[15] These tapes would play a surprising part in my version of the **Doctor Who** titles, because we would re-use them for our own work and, as you will discover later, accidentally failing to erase one of them properly, resulted in a really happy accident.

arrive home to be greeted by a trailer playing on the television. It would be advertising the very adventure that you'd just left unfinished at work!

Glastonbury

Mud and Glory

We're playing Glastonbury today.

Let's just say that again. We're playing Glastonbury today.

We get ferried from the entrance in a Range Rover. There's already a lot of mud, and our progress is slow. Whenever there's a crossing for the thousands of festival goers, a steward stops the flow of people, to let us through. By the looks on their faces, they are questioning why someone they don't recognise should have the luxury of a Range Rover.

Up above us to the left, on a high and sprawling hill, are pitched hundreds of tents. It's a canvas city, and we are slowly making our way down one of the main streets towards the Glade Stage. As you might imagine, this is not anything approaching the size of the Main Stage, which in a way comes as a relief. It seems in keeping with the size of our operation. The stage is covered, which is to be expected, but here the audience is also protected from the elements. This will come in very useful later on.

We introduce ourselves to the stage director, who discusses how we'll be able to set up around the other acts performing that day.

After a short burst of unpacking and rough positioning of gear, we have a few hours at our disposal to wander the site, before returning later to finish our preparation.

Glastonbury is every bit as impressive as you might expect. First of all, it covers a very wide area of land, with the stages set out along the bottom of a valley, and the space for campers spread out over the hills. The weather's not terrible, but there has been a good bit of rain already, and my boots sink into the mud as I trudge around.

The whole area is divided into main and lesser side routes. The main thoroughfares carry a constant stream of people, their footsteps hampered by the soft mud, which causes them to look down as they walk. Displaced people trudging through a strange landscape.

I make it back to the Glade Stage, where the final setup is in progress, involving the use of several rostra, or trucks on wheels. The gear is assembled on these floating islands behind a backdrop, and when the time's right, it's wheeled downstage into view. I test my setup. My footswitch and pedalboard are not working. There's already quite a buzz from the audience, and I'm using sign language to Mark, to tell him that we are not ready to go. I panic as much as the next person for any reason, at any time, but standing on a stage at Glastonbury with no means of putting on a show is a catastrophe of such massive proportions that panic is wholly insufficient. To my surprise, I discover that beyond panic there's a sort of calm resolve. I suppose it's borne out of the threat of impending embarrassment and the knowledge that methodically working through the gear to discover the fault is the only option. I find the fault with only a couple of minutes to spare.

It's then that the rain, which had held off for a while, starts again. A core amount of supporters and fans would always have been there, but the onset of the rain has caused a whole swathe of floating voters to seek shelter in the nearest available place. This does us a good turn, and swells the audience to capacity, with some of them half in and half out of the shelter. The sound's contained in the covered space, and the number of people deadens the acoustic. Ideal for our varied material; loud one moment and soft the next.

We launch into the set.

There's a very good feeling this time. You can sense that the audience is with you, enjoying the experience. The rain stops and the sun comes out, but the audience stays put, that's a good sign.

In every concert, there's always a sense of anticipation. '*Surely they're going to play it*'. It gets later and later, and still they're hoping it'll be the next number.

When deciding to hit the road as a band, it was a given that we had to play Ron Grainer's **Doctor Who** theme, and down the end of the concert seemed like a good idea. But like all pieces of specially written title music, the theme as written by Grainer would barely last two minutes. Luckily, a year or so before all this kicked off, I'd written a prequel to the theme that I'd called 'Before Who'.

I'd made up this rather far fetched narrative. If the 1980 version was taken as a fully evolved beast, how would that have sounded in embryonic form, and how would the creature have changed over time? So, I started with the sounds of some primeval slime[1] and threw around some tiny hints of the melody. Sometimes, just two or three notes, and even then played on an almost pitch-less sound, moving around in space. Very gradually short phrases from the theme would appear briefly and disappear just as fast.

---

[1] As many of you synthesiser users will have discovered, primeval slime is not a problem, anything else is somewhat harder.

Only after some time, as if delivered by a colliding meteor, the first Dum dee Dum bass arrived; but with even beats… Dum Dum Dum. Way in the distance, the Oo eee Oo is just a hint, slow and reverberant. In this way the theme was gradually constructed, but never played. Instead, a variation. Recognisable, but a variation nonetheless. After six and a half minutes, we are left hanging in space with the chord that will lead us into the sting, to be sharply followed by the full 1980 version of the **Doctor Who** theme.

So, when we set about discussing how to deliver **Doctor Who** in concert, 'Before Who', seemed an ideal lead in. Another thing that made it an even more exciting prospect for concert goers was the fact that across the whole six and half minutes, the tempo increases. As you can imagine, this builds a sense of anticipation, and by the time we launch into the 1980 theme, it acts as a form of release, and the audience really feel that they've got their money's worth.

There's something uncanny, hearing the **Doctor Who** theme at a rock festival. At every venue, there has always been a surge of extra people joining the audience. And so it is here at Glastonbury. The final explosion morphs into screams and applause, and they go away with smiles on their faces.

Timelines

That one tune established the department's reputation, but it was a tiny portion of our output. The whole of **Doctor Who** only accounted for about twelve percent of the total.

There are eleven thousand seven hundred and thirty-three project[2] entries in the Workshop's entire history. I have a database of over three thousand five hundred entries describing individual cues of music. Using

---

[2] A 'project' normally equates to a programme. Each project will contain any number of individual pieces, called 'cues'.

an average number of cues per project, and using that measurement across all the composers at the Workshop, results in a startling seventeen thousand five hundred individual items in total.

Working at the Workshop was a solitary activity, and it was sometimes easy to forget the work being done by other members of the department. There were as many timelines as there were composers; behind every closed door, a different series of projects was unfolding.

Despite the vast quantity of output, and the fact that each of us occupied what could be described as a parallel universe, some of my colleagues' work was hard to ignore.

In 1977 Malcolm Clarke[3] embarked on what would become a truly original production, *August 2026: There Will Come Soft Rains*[4], an adaptation of a short story by Ray Bradbury.

For me, it was the point at which I realised two important things.

1. Sometimes the best material you'll get from a new device is when you first take it out of the box.
2. The mixture of one voice and electronics is a powerful medium[5].

Malcolm Clarke directed the actor[6] who played the narrator, he wrote the adaptation of the short story, he composed and played all the music, and designed the manipulation of the robot voices that are scattered throughout.

We are in a house, where the machines that were designed to look after the owner, carry on long after he has died in a nuclear holocaust. In a

---

[3] Malcolm's 'Radiophonic Memoir' can be found on Ray White's site at https://whitefiles.org/rwm/index.htm
[4] First heard on BBC Radio 4 on 11 May, 1977.
[5] I would use that idea later when I wrote *Inferno Revisited*.
[6] The voice actor, Garard Green.

long mesmeric sequence, the voice of one of them opens the drama. To start with, all we hear is a bed of shifting sounds that slowly coalesce into recognisable speech. One or two syllables become audible, but it's still incoherent; almost inebriated.

To achieve this, Malcolm was moving a single control on the big EMS Vocoder labelled 'Freeze'. This control was not a switch but a knob which could slowly morph between a frozen vowel sound and a complete electronic rendition of a voice.

Little by little, words slide into our consciousness, and after a sequence that takes minutes to evolve, we hear:

"Today is August 4th, 2026."

We'd only taken delivery of the Vocoder a short time before, and because it had no means of remembering its settings, everything had to be performed in real time onto multitrack tape.

That great start to *August 2026* could never have been imagined in advance, it only became possible because of the equipment and the composer working as a team.

Malcolm Clarke won awards[7] for his work, and deservedly so. *August 2026*, created and produced in 1977, showed how genuine originality trumps quick-fix solutions any day. It still serves as a mission statement for the Radiophonic Workshop.

Of all the perfect matches between programme and composer, *The Hitchhiker's Guide to the Galaxy* must be up at the top of the list. Paddy Kingsland, the director Geoffrey Perkins, and the quite unique material

---

[7] *Society of Authors Award for Radio Drama* and the *Imperial Tobacco Award* 1977 (now the Sony Award).

from Douglas Adams bonded like they were made for each other.

I would have loved to have done this series, but it wouldn't have been as good if I had. Paddy's music has an immediate appeal that's hard to beat; a perfect match for the wonderful *HHGTTG*. The helicopter hovering over the rioting inhabitants of a planet with nothing but shoe shops, appealing to them to 'relax and enjoy their shoes', stays with you.

I'd first come across *HHGTTG* in a rather bizarre way, before the series ever appeared on the radio...

My pre-BBC musical associate John Ferdinando and I had long cherished the idea of writing scripts for radio comedy.

(Yes, I promise this is about *The Hitchhiker's Guide to the Galaxy*).

We'd written many sketches for a series of shows we staged at Ditchling and Lewes in Sussex from 1970 to 1975, a lot of which had gone down well. We rather fancied our chances at writing for BBC Light Entertainment. So, we set about assembling about half an hour's material in script form and I wrote to the Head of Light Entertainment, Simon Brett[8]. It was an internal memo rather than a letter from outside, and it got a reply immediately, which invited us both to see him in Broadcasting House.

We were excited about our prospects as comedy writers and appeared in his office, brandishing our half an hour of material.

I'd wondered how he would absorb so much copy in just one interview, but I needn't have worried. I'd never seen anyone speed-read until then. His eyes took up a position in the centre of the page and moved downwards, taking in the words to the left and right in his peripheral vision. As he did, he would give us immediate feedback on our jokes.

---

[8] You may know him in his more recent guise as a very successful author of murder mysteries. **The Charles Paris Mysteries** and many others.

"That's good."

"I like that."

"That doesn't work."

"No."

He finished the script and looked up.

"How long did it take you to write all this?" he asked.

We looked at one another.

"Oh, about a couple of months," we replied, knowing that it might have been even longer than that.

"There's some good stuff here and there, but you'd be expected to turn in something like this in about ten days, and then there would be rewrites."

This was way out of our league. I looked down in some embarrassment.

"I don't think we could manage that sort of turn around," I said.

After some slightly apologetic goodbyes, we left Simon Brett to his meteoric career, and headed down in the lift. Right down.

There was a cardboard box full of scripts in the corner of his office. It had been labelled "Star Trap".

I was convinced that 'Star Trap' had been a tongue-in-cheek reference to **Star Trek** and had been a working title for Douglas Adams' *Hitchhikers*. The timing was just too good to ignore, because a few weeks after our visit to the Head of Light Entertainment (Radio), Paddy Kingsland started work on the *The Hitchhiker's Guide to the Galaxy*.

I carried on thinking that for a great number of years. In fact, I'm rather embarrassed to admit that it was only when doing some research for this book, that I discovered (as fans of Simon Brett's novels will already know) that 'Star Trap' is one of his Charles Paris novels, and I'd seen a box containing early drafts.

Having removed any possible link to *HHGTTG*, I'll take up my rightful place as one of its fans; and there was a growing number of them at BBC Maida Vale. People carrying coffees back from the canteen, trudging up that endless corridor would linger outside Room 13[9] for months to come. Some marvellous stuff would seep out through the door of Paddy's studio.

If only Marvin had taken that off its hinges as well as destroying the wall, we would have heard it a lot better.

We play an excerpt from the series at almost every concert. It goes down well in every venue at home and abroad.

Malcolm and Paddy's work succeeded because it was fresh and original. Something that was becoming harder to achieve. In the early days, when all the gear was plundered from elsewhere or homemade, originality was guaranteed. With the gradual onset of marketed synthesisers, though, we faced easy options. Ready-made sounds or presets were available at the touch of a button, and when faced with tight deadlines, they were hard to resist.

Keyboards on synths had given an instant method of pitching, and now the off-the-shelf sound library caused further drift away from the unexpected. Perhaps, at long last, the machines were taking over; but if

---

[9] Now the name of our record label.

that was so, then the Workshop had to resist. The department's future relied on it.

I suppose it was a mixture of this need to keep fresh and a good deal of competitiveness that encouraged me to embark on what started out as a vanity project.

There was a good reason to want to do it. I felt there might have been some assumptions made about how I fitted in, especially by the head of the department, Desmond Briscoe.

Whilst Roger was busy writing songs for Children's TV and Paddy was delivering some really modern and memorable title music, it seemed to me that I was regarded as a slightest less attractive option to both of them. Not bad, but nothing special.

Part of my concern was that although I used guitar, and had composed with a guitar before joining the BBC, I was equally able on a piano. I say 'equally able', I wasn't very able on either of them, but at least what little dexterity I had, was evenly spread.

I needed a project that gave me a chance of composing in long form using a keyboard.

The album *Though a Glass Darkly* would be that project.

Through a Glass Darkly (In the Kingdom of Colours)	August 1977	BBC Enterprises	BBC Records
Life at Stake	August 1977	TV Science Features	BBC1
World About Us: Korea	September 1977	General Features	BBC2

Space Poetry Music	September 1977	WP06 Education	Radio Wales
Let's Move	November 1977	Features, Art & Education	Radio 4 Schools

There were twelve swing doors between my Radiophonic studio and Maida Vale Studio 4 (MV4) downstairs. I remember with such clarity because of the number of times late at night I'd struggle through them carrying the ARP synthesiser. The piano in the Workshop was OK for occasional use, but I wanted my solo album with BBC Records to feature the piano throughout the first side of the LP, and it had to be the Steinway. To this day, I have an uneasy relationship with fire doors, despite their obvious benefits; to me, they are still the enemy.

Playing and recording such an extensive piece was a challenge, but it had to be carried out whilst composing for my 'normal' job.

To be honest, I can't remember how it came about. Did I negotiate all those swing doors to make a demo for BBC Records, or were they involved earlier? The sheer exhaustion of it all seems to have obliterated some pertinent facts. This exhaustion was made harder still by the way that I had to work in MV4. The studio was designed for rock bands. A classy control room[10], with the latest SSL mixing desk and a 16 track Studer recorder. The studio, accessible through yet another set of swing doors, was furnished with a Steinway, a Hammond organ, amps, and some percussion. I was trying to record this without the help of an engineer. This was a solo endeavour. So I had to gauge how long it would take me to start the multitrack recorder, get through those double doors, leg it to the piano, put on the headphones, and try to remember what it was I was going to play in the first place.

On average, I'd give myself a minute and a half to get to the piano. I

---

[10] The BBC preferred to call the control room a 'cubicle', which always struck me as rather lavatorial, and completely unnecessary.

recorded a short section, alternating between a couple of tracks; each time trying to improve on the previous take. In the end, I'd then have the luxury of mixing the best performances from each track, and bounce them down to a third, which would become the piano master.

I'd decided that the piece should be allegorical. The piano represented the main character, the protagonist who stood for 'good'. The character's journey through the piece represents the triumph of good over evil, a journey through a landscape that was forever changing and challenging. The piece was to be called 'In the Kingdom of Colours'.

I'd like you now to picture the scene as I tried to pitch this idea to BBC Records.

I'm invited into Mike Harding's office. Mike is a no nonsense Glaswegian, with plenty of experience in bringing music to the BBC's record buying public. His experience of 'allegory' however is less clear.

Opposite him now is this effete young man from a department rumoured to be elitist and full of madmen, talking about protagonists and the triumph of good over evil. It does not bode well. Mike, who'd listened to the piece and taken it at face value, was now being told it meant something, and was having doubts. He resorted to changing the easiest thing first, the name. 'In the Kingdom of Colours' smacked of twee-ness and pretension, he wanted something more direct.

To my surprise he said, "I've often found that quotes from the Bible make good album titles."

Over the next few days, we exchanged Bible quotes and settled on 'Through a Glass Darkly'[11]. I'm still disappointed that my original title never made it. It might have been twee and even pretentious, but it planted the idea of travelling through a landscape, which was an important part

---

[11] 1 Corinthians 13:12

of the concept. Still, the album could have been called 'The Whore of Babylon'[12], so I probably got off lightly.

Side Two of the album contained a selection of compositions not associated with any narrative: 'Caches of Gold', 'Magenta Court', 'Colour Rinse', 'Wind in the Wires', and 'The Astronauts'.

Magenta Court

Few people realise that 'Magenta Court' is named after a block of flats.

I used to walk from BBC Maida Vale in Delaware Road to a gym and swimming pool in Ladbroke Grove. I remember on one occasion sharing the pool with Angela Rippon. It was just her and me. She, gliding serenely along the surface of the pool, me making waves on the other side. I was walking back to work, musing on the fact that I'd just shared the pool with a celebrity (at that moment she was clearly not thinking the same), when I passed an average block of flats called 'Magnolia Court'. In fact, they named all the flats around there after colours, Magnolia, Violet, and Magenta. I'd already started work on the piece and hadn't got a title for it, so I used 'Magenta Court'. It had associations with 'The Court of the Crimson King' by King Crimson, whilst being decidedly tongue in cheek. Less than serious titles featured in my pre BBC days when working with John Ferdinando and H&F Recordings, and a solo album seemed a good place to revive the idea. The piece also re-appeared on an exercise video for the Green Goddess[13] some time afterwards, and now gets a rockier airing in our concerts.

Colour Rinse

This was an out-and-out piece of seventies synthesiser pop (and sounds horribly dated today). The idea was that after listening to the A side

---
[12] Revelation 17:3–18
[13] Diana Moran, who presented a famous exercise section on the BBC's **Breakfast Time** show in the early 1980s.

called 'In the Kingdom of Colours', you'd need to 'rinse out the colours' by listening to this piece of synthetic fun. After Mike Harding's insistence on changing the name of the album, the whole plan fell apart.

Wind In the Wires

This was a number written and recorded in my studio in Hove, Sussex, shortly after I'd joined the BBC. I was still finishing a solo album under the H&F Recordings label[14], as well getting to grips with my new job as a Studio Manager. It was achieved using track bouncing between two Revox stereo tape recorders, and it's rather pleasing to see it alongside all the other tracks recorded in the far better equipped BBC studios. Even more satisfying to know that German broadcasting used it on one of their regular programmes for many years.

The Astronauts

It seemed like an ideal opportunity to present a longer version of the track for the album, so the opening of 'The Case of the Ancient Astronauts' was spliced onto the 'B' Side of my 1980 **Doctor Who** theme. They were made for one another!

Of course, expecting one piece on an album to alter how I was regarded was wishful thinking. How we are all regarded evolves over time. Writers are constantly told to 'show, don't tell' and the same applied here. In the creative industries, you often hear the phrase '*You're only as good as your last work.*" While this might be the case when it comes to directors commissioning their next composer, it does not apply to a gradually acquired reputation. To achieve that, you need a body of work and that doesn't happen overnight.

Towards the end of the seventies, thanks to the persistence of our organiser, Brian Hodgson, the department got its own annual budget. It

---

[14] The track appears on H&F's fifth album *Friends*.

was a long time coming, but transformed the equipping of the studios. Effective communication between pieces of gear was still some way off and so new equipment was haphazardly added to the old and the studio was more cluttered than ever.

Fire regulations were more relaxed at the time, which is just as well, because my exit from this nest of technology was a long and winding road. It was made worse by the occasional arrival of the Fairlight trolley. If it hadn't been used to support the most valuable piece of hardware in the department, it would have been dispensing teas. Far from custom built, it had wheels that constantly bent sideways on the many ramps between my studio and the others.

In time, all this equipment would communicate and the control would be centralised, but for now, there was a buzz about sitting amongst this Aladdin's cave of possibilities.

The One Show

Duct Tape

We are playing on BBC1's **The One Show** tonight.

Ours is to be one of the last shows coming from their old studio in White City London. First of all they want to put us on the roof. It's winter. We protest that the gear won't work in that cold, which is true, but we are really referring to ourselves. They give in, and we are able to set up down one end of a rather small studio, no bigger than a double garage. Mark and Dick are being interviewed and the rest of us are there to play.

This studio's not, and never has been, geared to music. It's a speech studio, and the whole thing is a tight squeeze. Matt Baker and Alex Jones are unflappable and highly professional, but without the skill of the Floor Manager neither we, nor the rest of the contributors, would have the slightest idea what's happening. He seems to be carrying the whole thing. Mark's set to demonstrate the wonderful early synthesiser, the Korg MS20, on camera, and he and Matt Baker practise the piece. During it, Mark mentions that some of our early music has just been reissued.

"*Wow,*" Matt says, with slightly false enthusiasm. "*On cassette, I assume!*"

Our presence here is clearly for nostalgic reasons.

There's a dressing room set aside for the programme guests. There are ourselves, Sir Bruce Keogh (a leading cardiac surgeon), a lady with a hi-tech prosthetic leg, and two Cybermen. It's hard enough to talk sequentially about such disparate subjects on air, but tipping them in the same room to chat amongst themselves just seems to be pure farce.

Sir Bruce has yet to appear, but the rest of us flay around, trying to make polite conversation. The only thing we have in common is that none of us are racing drivers, but that doesn't seem to help. At last, the tension is somewhat relieved by the two guys who are playing the Cybermen deciding to change into their costumes. They get into the suits easily enough but one of the helmets is causing some trouble. It seems to be riding up off the collar, leaving a gap around the neck. It isn't really the guy's neck that's the problem, it's more that his friend hasn't got a neck and that explains why his helmet has settled down and this one hasn't.

Kieron Pepper, our drummer, has just the thing. All drummers have a selection of hardware to maintain their kit, and Kieron produces some duct tape out of his bag. Being grey, it's ideal, and after a minute or two he has taped the helmet to the collar of the suit and everyone, grateful for something talk about, agrees that it works a treat.

At the given time, we assemble down at the end of the studio and the programme goes on air. It's the usual rag bag of impossible segues and lucky dip pieces that fill the seven o'clock slot, including an interview with Sir Bruce, the more serious guest, who's been invited to talk about the NHS.

I'm sitting at the synthesiser keyboard at the edge of the space devoted to the band, and immediately alongside me is the lady with the hi-tech prosthetic leg who has already featured in an earlier item. It quite surprised me that by a clever use of close ups the band were never revealed during her piece, despite being as tightly packed as a commuter train.

Suddenly, without warning, there's the most almighty crash. Not just one, more like a cascade of crashes. I look towards Kieron, who's desperately trying to hold on to his kit as bits of it tumble in all directions. A Cyberman's helmet appears on the floor. I can see it quite clearly through the lady's prosthetic leg which, because of its construction from high tensile modern materials, is an open weave of struts and supports. The Cyberman's helmet lies there inert. It takes me a few seconds to realise that the rest of the Cyberman is still in it. That duct tape has worked well. So well that it has completely sealed the guy inside. His supply of oxygen being limited, and the studio being rather hot, there came a point at which something had to give and he has passed out. But rather than go straight down, he clearly wanted to take out something on the way; and who better than the bastard who sealed him in that suit in the first place.

Matt Baker, who seems to be able to turn every occasion to his advantage, explains what's happened.

"You might have heard a loud noise just then, but it's OK, it's just one of our Cybermen who has fainted."

This must have come as a shock to the viewing public who, firstly, hadn't even seen any Cybermen yet, and secondly, now knew that their enjoyment of them had already been cut by fifty percent.

"But don't worry," Matt continues, *"we've just the man to go to his assistance. Sir Bruce Keogh of the NHS."*

Sir Bruce duly attends to the patient over our side of the studio, as another guest is led in. To my surprise, it's Sir John Hurt. Now looking very frail and elderly, but unmistakably the actor so many of us admire.

He makes his way to the sofa and his interview begins.

They certainly pack quite a lot into the half-hour programme. We are due to play at the end of the show, and, when the time comes round, put in a passable performance, but I think we all know what the outcome will be.

If you are to ask anyone now whether they remember it, they'll probably say no, until you remind them that it was the show when the Cyberman fainted. They will have forgotten Sir Bruce Keogh, the lady with the hi-tech prosthetic leg, Sir John Hurt, and the Radiophonic Workshop, but the Cyberman who passed out on the drum kit lives on. For a while afterwards, the guy who collapsed was so certain of his immortality that he had his own Twitter account[1].

---

[1] @faintingcyberman, naturally.

Part 2

Investing in Our Future

RADIOPHONIC TIMES

Polyphonic

Most electronic sound sources would only play one pitch at a time, and re-pitching sound was laborious, and harmonies hard won. Early synths might have introduced a whole raft of other sounds, but were still only capable of a single played pitch.

So, with the advent of polyphonic synthesisers[1], there was considerable rejoicing in many quarters, but some misgivings in others. For some, sitting at a keyboard to deliver music in the same way that you would sit at a piano was a retrograde step.

Mono synthesisers had already given us a world devoid of effort. And effort was at the heart of what had gone before; not just in the composers themselves, but also in the sounds they were creating.

Delia's **Doctor Who** theme does indeed sound as if this music is being formed mysteriously out of a great deal of effort. These strange elemental sounds, with their competing harmonics, make a shifting, ephemeral

---

[1] Which could play chords, ie. more than one note at a time.

music. Effort is at the heart of classical sounds that we hear every day. A violin note is created by the friction of a bow across a string, and the resulting sound is rich with complicated harmonics. A flute note is formed when air's blown across the mouthpiece and excites a resonance in the body of the instrument. A horn player will literally blow a raspberry into the mouthpiece of a French Horn to set up a vibrating current of air resulting in a note. And then along comes the synthesiser which, even in its mono form, delivered a sound that seemed effortless, because of its purity. No complicated harmonics here. Even the more intricate electronic waveforms didn't get close.

The one area that had given that effortless sound some random ingredients was in the creation of chords. Now, with the arrival of polyphony, even the effort of making harmony had been removed.

When I produced 'The Astronauts', each chord had to be built up note by note on the ARP Odyssey, and it took hours of work. These polyphonic synths were capable of delivering a very similar result in an instant. Also, the old technique of layering chords one note at a time would result in differences in start time, attack and duration, which might not be present in the polyphonic version.

This was a new situation that needed special consideration, but we were excited all the same, because we would be able to take on bigger projects.

Of course, all of this didn't happen in an instant, and despite the availability of synth polyphony, and our own budget, the Workshop wouldn't be able to play enough notes at the same time for a little while yet!

It would take a rather special project to persuade the management that this move towards more musical polyphonic synths was worthwhile.

The Body in Question

Coping with Emergencies	April 1978	Current Affairs	Radio 4 Woman's Hour
Straight Down the Line	July 1978	Radio 4	Radio 4
Radio 4 Logo	June 1978	TV Presentation	Radio 4
History Series	July 1978	World Service	External Services
Radio Newsreel	July 1978	World Service	External Services
Sports Round Up	July 1978	World Service	External Services
The Body in Question Eps 1 to 13	August 1978	TV Science Features	BBC2

Desmond Briscoe, Head of the Workshop, liked a tidy desk when he went home in the evening; no unresolved matters for the next day. Over the years, he had applied that rule more and more rigorously. So, when a call came through from Patrick Uden around midday, asking for someone to provide his TV series with some simple music to accompany a cell dividing, the 'Hot Potato Routine' swung into action.

As soon as the phone had been put down, the race was on to find someone to take on the project. By pure chance, I was passing his office door at that very moment.

"Something's just come in," he called out. "I thought you might like to do it."

I stepped into his office.

"It's not very much, just a one off."

It certainly didn't seem to be very much. In fact, it reminded me of my very first project at the Radiophonic Workshop, the flying steak and kidney pie. Still, it wouldn't take very long to do.

It turned out to be my first contact with **The Body in Question**, a thirteen-part series about human biology written and presented by Jonathan Miller, and produced by Patrick Uden.

Indeed, this initial request was a quick job, but by the time I'd finished it, Patrick had been on the phone again with something else. And so it continued, the jobs becoming increasingly more musical as time went on. After a while, I'd done enough for there to be a house style, a certain ethos to the films that was consistent. At this point Patrick decided to throw in his lot with me and asked whether I wanted to do the whole thirteen-part series. It was an immediate 'yes' from me. In fact, I regarded it as an honour to work on such a prestigious project.

When I first joined the Workshop, there had been much talk about a previous series. **The Ascent of Man** was a science-based series written and presented by Jacob Bronowski. It had established a thirst in the TV audience for being taken on a journey of exploration by the country's leading scientists. Given the graphic possibilities of the medium, surprisingly complex ideas could be illustrated in amazing detail. The audience were being treated as intelligent beings who were interested in a challenging subject, and capable of understanding it.

The premise of **The Body in Question** followed the same successful formula. There were to be thirteen hour-long episodes, each dealing with a different topic. They would be written and presented by the polymath Jonathan Miller[2]. Just as in the case of Bronowski and **The Ascent of**

---

[2] Wikipedia describes Miller as 'an English theatre and opera director, actor, author, television presenter, humorist, and medical doctor'.

Man, The Body in Question would be a series of personal explorations, this time on the subject of human biology and our attitudes to our own physiology. Also similar to its predecessor, this was not to be a dry treatise, but a lively and entertaining journey. Miller's experience in the theatre and in music was to be the driving force behind the presentation of his ideas. Something that also enriched my experience of the project.

The thirteen episodes took a massive fourteen months to complete. Over that time, I was to compose an hour and a half of music. When all the work was done, Patrick sent Desmond Briscoe a memo[3]. He referred back to the music's small beginnings and how it had mushroomed, 'It grew like Topsy,' he said.

Film Confetti

Perhaps fourteen months may seem excessive to us today, but the technology we had at our disposal was nothing like as swift and easy to use. Just being able to view the programme we were scoring was, by today's standards, a hit and miss affair. First of all, there needed to be a reliable way to make sure that what you were writing would match the length of the sequence in the programme. **The Body in Question** was being shot entirely on film. Video was only used for studio-based shows, with occasional interjections of film clips when the action went outside. Old comedy shows are a good example of this, where the quality would shift from video to film and back again. Because this whole series was being filmed, Jonathan Miller's pieces to camera would also be on film, and were shot on a specially designed set in the BBC Ealing studios. Once all the material was shot, it would be assembled and edited in one of two cutting rooms. Using two of them allowed for a greater period of work on every programme of the series. At various stages in this editing process, I'd be sent short clips or scenes from the shows, allowing me to

---

[3] An internal letter sent through the BBC's own internal postal service. These days, of course, it would be an email. These complimentary memos which happened occasionally after successful projects were referred to in the department as 'herograms'.

start work on the music. These clips would be on 16mm film with an accompanying 16mm magnetic sprocketed soundtrack, both playable on a Steenbeck (a large film viewer the size of a kitchen table). This machine would occupy the so-called film room, a small space off the main top corridor of BBC Maida Vale. There was only one of these film viewers to be shared by all the composers in the department.

Writing this now, I've several times had to refer back to confirm that it really was that laborious. It seems incredible that all of the ninety minutes of music for **The Body in Question** (and indeed any synced music of the period) was only achievable using such an imprecise and clumsy method. No wonder it took me fourteen months.

Having taken delivery of the film clips (usually by a courier on a motorbike), I would go down to the film room, and whilst looking at the material, would note down the locations of all the cue-points for a piece of music. Having previously agreed with the director where the music would occur, it was my job to plan out the important moments (such as cuts or action) in each piece of music. All this was measured in 16mm film feet. I'd end up with a list of these locations, which would then have to be converted into minutes and seconds. This list would then be taken back to the studio and work would commence.

Before starting a piece of music, I used to record an audio timecode onto track eight of the multitrack. This would consist of a recording of my voice reciting seconds from zero up to half an hour. This was an audio ruler against which I could record the music on the other seven tracks.

Once I was happy with the result, I'd take a mix from the multitrack (a 1/4 inch stereo tape) to the Film Unit up the corridor. In one of their rooms, there was a single stereo machine to play the music and a so-called Mag Track Recorder. This would copy my tape onto a 16mm magnetic track[4], which could then be laid against the film clip back in our film

---

[4] Sprocketed magnetic recording tape the same size as the film.

room. Only then would I see if the music I was writing fitted the film. If it didn't, or was unsuitable, I'd have to note down things to change, return to my studio and work towards an improved version, which would once again have to be transferred to 16mm.

The Mag Track recorder in the Film Unit was a vicious beast. It stood vertically in an equipment bay. The spool of sprocketed tape and its empty take-up spool were secured to the machine by a metal centre hub which was screwed into position once the new tape had been installed. On one occasion, whilst fast winding back to the beginning, the hub shot out from its mooring, flew across the room, and embedded itself in the acoustic tiles on the opposite wall. It was almost midnight, there were very few people in the building and I wondered what would have happened if, instead of the wall, it had embedded itself into my head.

The film viewer in our film room was just as temperamental.

Fast winding was always a long and boring process. Leaving the room whilst the film spun back was always tempting, and I remember one time when it was a good half an hour before I remembered I had left it unattended. I wasn't prepared for what I saw when I returned. It had completed its rewind, and since there was no automatic stop on the machine, continued to revolve at high speed for many minutes. During this time, the end of the film had whipped out from the spool, eventually reaching an angle poise lamp, the arm of which sliced off a six inch length of film on every revolution. These short pieces of film had flown across the room, and because they were now charged with static, stuck themselves to all the walls. Hundreds of pieces of film on the ceiling, walls and floor. It had eaten so far into the film, that I'd successfully destroyed the entire first scene. We lived dangerously in those days.

Once all the cues[5] for a programme were complete, I'd take them to the cutting room on Mag Track tape ready to be viewed on their Steenbeck

---

[5] Individual pieces of music.

with the editor and producer, and then finally delivered to the dubbing suite where the finished audio for the entire programme would be produced.

A machine room alongside the dubbing theatre would house many Mag Track playback machines. These would contain all the different ingredients of the soundtrack: the commentary, sounds, and of course the music. All these machines had to stay in sync to the frame. When one machine arrived at a certain frame, then all the others needed to be in exactly the same place. Sadly, when travelling fast, these machines would drop frames and lose sync. This meant that once we'd attempted a mix of a scene, and had decided to do it again, we'd have to watch the whole scene spool backwards at normal speed to preserve synchronisation.

As you can imagine, **The Body in Question** featured quite a few disturbing scenes. It was one of the first programmes to cover hospital operations and in programme thirteen, even an autopsy. Because we were viewing so called ungraded film during our work, the colours were rather vivid. Especially the greens and reds. There's quite a lot of green and a great deal of red in an operation, and we were forced to see these time and time again, as they inched backwards at normal speed. In order to avoid nausea, as soon as the machines started their slow crawl back to the beginning, we all set about chatting to one another. These conversations, sometimes rather desperate, were conducted in two minute bursts throughout the day. One popular dubbing mixer was a keen collector of porcelain, and would hold forth on his favourite subject at the drop of a hat. It was a strange experience, concentrating on the film for two minutes, chatting idly for another two, and then when we were ready, moving to the next scene until the whole programme's soundtrack had been completed.

The Dream Machine

There's one synthesiser that seems to have been associated with me over the years. One that Vangelis had already made his own.

It was during **The Body in Question** that I first came across the Yamaha CS80. I'd been present at a demonstration of the machine, and I liked the ease with which you could perform changes to the sounds, both by using very smooth tabs (a little like on a Hammond organ), but also by passing your finger up and down a long velvet strip above the keyboard. This touch strip, which has never been bettered since, allowed the performance of spontaneous pitch and modulation changes. By resting your thumb on it and then using the fingers of the same hand, you could simulate the fingering of a violin string.

Despite our newly acquired budget, we were not able to buy expensive new equipment on a whim. The refurbishment of all the studios at the Workshop could not be an instant fix, and the CS80 was pricey, almost £5000. Luckily, Patrick Uden suggested that the programme budget might allow us to hire equipment. So, I persuaded him to hire me a CS80.

Each of the thirteen programmes required a few weeks' work, and the synthesiser was brought in specially for each occasion. This was a big machine, Maida Vale had a long corridor, and my studio was halfway down. I like to think it was by coincidence, but for the first seven or eight occasions I was not at the Workshop when the synthesiser arrived. When I got to work, whoever had the job of helping the unwieldy thing down to my studio, made their feelings quite clear.

By the last quarter of the series, the BBC had allowed us to buy one of our own. There had already been some musical successes in the opening programmes and it was obvious that the machine would enhance the Workshop's output.

I've since found out that the CS80 that I played at the Workshop was subsequently sold to the composer Michael Price[6], who used it to great

---

[6] Who also composed the music for **Sherlock**, and **Unforgiven** on ITV.

effect on **Dracula** in 2020 for the BBC. He first suspected that it had been mine when he opened the tuning compartment on the top left of the machine. This housed tiny replicas of the main controls which you could use to memorise[7] different settings. Attached to one of these was a post-it note which read '*PH Please Leave 21/1/84*'. Around this time I was working on the third and fourth episodes of the **Doctor Who** adventure *Planet of Fire* and must have been nervous that someone would alter the settings before I finished the music.

The Greenwich Chorus

There was to be a sequence in episode 3 of **The Body in Question** referring to The Royal Society, with images of The Greenwich Observatory, and particularly John Flamsteed's clock. It was one of those occasions when Patrick Uden, Jonathan Miller and myself discussed the piece in some detail.

I was somewhat hesitant about writing it. It clearly had to have a classical feel, but also needed to feel part of the overall score, which featured some electronic material.

It was surprising to some that a series written and presented by a polymath such as Jonathan Miller, with his extensive knowledge of music history, should have a score by the Radiophonic Workshop. At no time, though, did I feel intimidated by Jonathan's enviable musical knowledge. With this cue, we faced the ancient or modern dilemma head on.

"*Perhaps a chorale might work, like Purcell?*" suggested Miller.

He must have thought it merely an incidental passing remark, but to me it was the catalyst which resulted in 'The Greenwich Chorus'. My head nodded, but I needed to find out what that sounded like. My early

---

[7] Like four mini copies of the controls, it simply allowed you to go back to previous settings. A long way from today's computer recall.

influences were often from classical music (Holst, Beethoven, Stravinsky etc) but Purcell was not in there anywhere. Some research was required. This was a long time before the likes of Spotify, so after a visit to the BBC Record Library and playing through a lot of Purcell's music I came across 'Rejoice in the Lord Alway, Z49'.

If you listen to this, you'll hear the highly melodic choral work, and also the trumpet sound, both of which found their way into the final piece. At this point I should make it clear that my sight reading[8] is not good enough to perform the score of 'Rejoice in the Lord alway' without a lot of work. This is a pity in a lot of situations, but an enormous benefit in others. I've never found it easy to copy any music at all, and have always relished originating everything myself. So, although I heard what the result might sound like, I knew that it would inevitably end up sounding like Howell rather than Purcell. Nevertheless, the idea of trumpets and melodic choral sounds did stick, and enabled me to start work on this piece, knowing it was similar to what had been suggested.

It was clear from the start that the Vocoder was going to be involved. I remember when it first appeared at the Workshop, heralded as a useful device to make a group of voices out of one. It did make a voice sound like several, but overlaid it with a kind of phased gloss, which was completely unsuitable for a real life drama, though a fascinating sound, nonetheless. And so it was with 'The Greenwich Chorus'. This was not to be a bad copy of Purcell, but hopefully something original in its own right.

So I started work. There was a recording of Flamsteed's Clock[9] made by the sound recordist at the shoot in the Greenwich Observatory. I laid that down onto one track of the multitrack. This piece was going to be at 60 beats per minute, the clock would see to that.

Using that as a metronome, I made vocal noises into a microphone whilst

---

[8] The ability to look at a score, and immediately play the music.
[9] This clock sound can be heard on the final piece.

playing chords on the synthesiser keyboard. I could hear the resulting electronic vocal harmonies through my headphones. Very soon it became clear what sort of melody would work given that tempo, and for reasons of convenience[10], the key of G major seemed to work well.

What followed was a long series of vocal experiments. Trying to make the robotic Vocoder sound like a chorus was an uphill struggle, and at that time you needed to do a complete pass perfectly, as editing multitrack tape was impractical. It was easier to just let the tape run until a good take was recorded. I have a digital transcription of the whole multitrack tape I used to make 'The Greenwich Chorus', and the final piece is a 45 second section in the middle of the tape. All the rest is filled with failed experiments. Since then I have come across more information about The Royal Society and one of its unsung heroes, Robert Hooke, who was 'Curator of Experiments'. He would have been proud of me.

In addition, I had the words to consider. I'd looked at quite a few librettos and had singled out some possible contenders. Often, though, they came with too many religious associations which were not appropriate for the sequence. In any case, it's not wise to put sung words behind a voice over. We're always drawn to listen to the words, and our attention is distracted away from the commentary[11].

I started to experiment with phonetic sounds instead. Amongst the many letters and emails I've received about 'The Greenwich Chorus', a few have made an attempt at deciphering the words. One person amusingly claimed to be able to hear 'Harry Secombe' in there somewhere. Others have laboriously worked out Latin verse to match the sounds. I can categorically say that I was uttering phonetics (ta pa sa etc), but I experimented with what worked best at various points. After many hours, I settled on the sounds and chords which would give that nice

---

[10] Mostly to do with a comfortable pitch for my voice. Although the actual pitch is not heard in the final product, it's easier to pitch live with a Vocoder if the sung pitch is at least in the chords that are playing.

[11] As we will see, despite my efforts, it happened anyway.

balance of melody and harmony. The actual sequence in the programme was about 45 seconds, and one pass of the melody worked well in that timeframe. So, now I was all set to start making the whole thing sound right. After all, there was no accompaniment to the voices apart from the clock sound.

I decided that we needed to hear the clock loud and clear from the outset. The clock on its own sounded too basic though, and so I decided to use a harpsichord figure to accompany it. The Workshop was littered with odd electronic keyboards that were cast-offs from other parts of the BBC. I can't even remember the name of this one, but I do know that it was only able to do three sounds; two simply awful organ sounds, and a very passable harpsichord. Having sorted the opening harpsichord flourish, it seemed only right to continue the harpsichord accompaniment throughout the piece. That inspired the addition of bass, flute-like arpeggios and the trumpet sound. All this started to show up the Vocoded choral lines I'd laid down to start with, and so I returned to those and re-performed them.

The result went down well with Jonathan and the producer, who tried to find other places in the programme where 'The Greenwich Chorus' could reappear.

Jamming the Switchboard

The events on the night of its first broadcast were unusual, to say the least.

It's difficult to say exactly how many calls it took to jam the BBC switchboard in 1978, but jammed it was. Having worked with BBC Radio 3, I know only too well the small number of communications required to constitute a 'flood of letters from listeners', so I treat this all with caution. Apparently though, so many viewers of **The Body in Question** were fascinated by the mysterious 'singing' in 'The Greenwich Chorus' that their calls caused a massive telephonic log jam. They'd rung because they thought they had heard a human voice but weren't sure, and the mystery needed clearing up as soon as possible. We are all programmed like that. We'll recognise the shape of a face in the middle of a complicated jumble of visual information, and similarly we are pre-programmed to decipher anything that might be a voice telling us something we need to hear. The message hidden in this music was unintelligible, it was never intended to be anything else, but they didn't know that. This goes to the heart of what interested people in our output in the first place. The fascination with the unknown and the original. Delia's **Doctor Who** title music had awakened a thirst in the audience to hear really new things, and to try to make sense of them, and although this piece had started its life as a nod towards Purcell, it had finished somewhere else entirely.

Sadly, Jonathan Miller died as I was writing this book, and during an obituary on Radio 3 'The Greenwich Chorus' was played.

Without Jonathan's gentleness and acceptance of my limited knowledge of classical music, that piece would have never been written, and my subsequent confidence and enthusiasm for writing music of any genre might never have blossomed. He was a conscientious man, surrounded by books even at the final mix of a programme, checking the facts. Keen not to let those people down who were still hard at work in the profession with which he still felt such a strong association.

The Lady in Latex

"How on earth do you get your ideas?"

A question often asked of composers.

I suppose the reason that we all smile weakly and try to think of an appropriate answer is that we don't know either. Ideas arrive without a detailed provenance, they come from associations, context, and a whole host of different triggers. Anyway, once you've got an idea, it's almost too late to work out where it's come from.

For me, dramatic and visual stimuli are important. Sometimes paintings or strange sculptures make me think of the relationship of sounds and musical phrases. I don't have a conventional musical approach to composition. Successive notes come from the music itself, rather than being forced into existence by a set of rules. This has resulted in work of all sorts, both conventional and experimental.

All very pretentious, I hear you mutter. Well, this technique comes with some serious downsides, most of which can be described in one word.

Deadlines.

If you're late delivering something, then two things are certain:

1. That director will never work with you again.
2. You're one step closer to losing your job.

Any inclination to be self indulgent and pretentious is forgotten in the headlong rush to 'get it done'. One thing that made the Radiophonic Workshop stand out from the other experimental studios of the period (including IRCAM[12] and others) was that it tried to innovate within the confines of tight deadlines. With time tight, lengthy sessions composing at the piano were rare, but on one occasion, it paid off.

I was living in a one bedroom flat in the Goldhawk Road, London. A busy road with constant traffic. The noise from outside was so great that the landlord had installed triple glazing. My piano was alongside the

---

[12] *Institut de Recherche et Coordination Acoustique/Musique*, in some ways our French counterpart.

window in the front room and I sat noodling[13] on it, not even expecting to write anything. Having said that visual stimuli are important to me, I can't imagine how the traffic on the Goldhawk Road inspired me to write the title music to **The Body in Question**, but anyway I started to play stepping chords that then led to me improvising a top line. It was as if I was sitting there teaching myself to play a piece that already existed; like the sculptor who says that he's chipping away at a large slab of stone until he discovers a statue that's been hiding inside all along.

I always get absorbed in what I'm doing, and after what seemed like about an hour, I realised I'd been working on it for three. By that time though, the stepping chords, the top line and the middle eight were all in place.

At work in Maida Vale the next day, I worked out how this pre-written piece could be played and produced, using the sounds at my disposal. As I've said, this was unusual, because normally the sounds themselves formed part of the writing process. Although I always wanted my material to have something special about it, I knew also that the ethos of this series would have a classical thread running through it, so some input from live musicians was necessary. Not only was Jonathan Miller a recognised musicologist and doctor, but many times in the series he would follow a subject from its inception centuries ago to the present day, and suitable period music would be appropriate anyway. So, I decided to use a flute and a cello, as well as sounds derived from my familiar palette of vocoder and synthesisers.

In the meantime, discussions got under way to come up with suitable visuals for the opening titles. A graphics designer joined the team and delivered one or two ideas. I'd already started the music and was able to let them hear an early mock-up to help with the discussion. There was a fashion to use 2D artwork together with unusual fonts to create titles, but this did not go down well with the director or presenter. They

---

[13] A very colloquial term used by musicians to describe the mindless stabbing of keys on an instrument, with no real end. Apart from a slight satisfaction in hearing that the instrument still works, and that you're irritating the hell out of anyone within earshot.

wanted something real, not fabricated, and they eventually hit on the idea of filming the human form. Early experiments were rejected as being plain and clumsy, and it would take many failed attempts before a solution was found.

Creative effects were limited at the time. Nowadays, with everything being reduced to the common language of the computer, almost anything is possible visually, as is clear from Hollywood's graphically rich feature films. During the eighties though, visual effects were often performed in front of the camera. Moving distortion, like a hall of mirrors, was achieved by shooting through a twisting sheet of perspex. Castles on distant hilltops could be added to a landscape by painting them on the top portion of a piece of glass and positioning it precisely in front of the camera. So, the **Body in Question** titles needed to use an actual body, but it had to be disguised. The solution would involve a tricky film shoot. They acquired a massive sheet of latex, stretched it over a large frame which looked a little like a tall bed frame, and lit it from below. In a secretive session (I only heard about it after it was finished) they had hired a naked model to move on top of this highly pliable sheet, whilst the camera filmed from the floor upwards. The result was a fascinating hint of a shifting human form[14] that never showed its entire shape at once, but offered the viewer a glimpse of various parts of the body that undulated with the music.

Audiences have become used to the unusual, and are a lot harder to please, but even today, the 'Lady in Latex' remains a wonderfully enigmatic sequence.

With the visuals finalised, the music recordings could go ahead. I'd chosen to use the cellist, Ross Pople, principal cello in the BBC Symphony Orchestra, and the flautist, Sebastian Bell, who played with the London Sinfonietta.

---

[14] The registered name of the opening music to The Body in Question that appears on all the programme documentation is 'Moving Form', inspired by the visuals.

Unfortunately, they were not available on the same day! Session fixers will choose the day and then find the musicians, but I was keen to have these two players, and so held two sessions. It gave me some extra work, but paid off in the end.

Mesmerised

In the course of my time at the Workshop, I was able to attend many TV and film shoots.

Many of them were intended to give me a glimpse of the style and content of the programme, but sometimes, if I'd prepared music to be played on set, I would be actively involved.

Jonathan Miller and Patrick Uden had decided to illustrate the activities of Anton Mesmer, a quack medic who used magnetism to 'cure' his patients.

The series had already established an entertaining presentation style, but this took it one stage further. Lindsay Kemp's mime group was commissioned. Their extrovert choreography would move to music of mine, played into the scene from loudspeakers.

With everything prepared, I turned up at Ealing Studios (then owned by the BBC) to oversee the playback.

I'm always struck by how run down and shabby most film studios are. They are basically weather proof empty shells. Ealing was no exception. The walls of the film stage looked as if, even on the day they were built, they were in serious need of attention. But it's the construction and lighting of the set built between these unpromising walls that really matters.

Patrick Uden and I had previously discussed the generic set for the series.

It would be used for a lot of Jonathan Miller's pieces to camera. Patrick was a great fan of grey; to him it was vital to select the right sort of grey, but grey it had to be. Although it seemed a drab idea, the result of course was to highlight anything of colour that was within the grey set, and it proved to be very effective.

We were still using the grey set on this occasion, but it had been transformed to represent Mesmer's 'surgery'. Lindsay Kemp and members of his troop were dressed in outrageous costumes of the period. One of them, Orlando, wore a ship on his head. At the height of the drama, he threw himself, his dress, and his ship into convulsions. Mesmer's magnetic therapy was more of an intense rite than it was healing.

But this was film and not video, and it was put together like any film, in a series of takes from different angles, that would be edited later. There's a precaution that film makers always take when filming to pre-recorded music. There has to be at least one shot that's the whole duration of the music, often a fairly wide one, that will act as a reference for the synchronisation of any cut away or different angles during the edit. However, in a piece of this length, it was just as easy to keep on playing through the whole piece. The artists had to work very hard as a result, and towards the end of the day, Orlando, his frock and his ship became progressively more dishevelled and Orlando himself less inclined to throw himself around with the same enthusiasm.

The music for this scene had been written with a certain narrative in mind; the assembling of the characters, the setting up of the magnetic apparatus, the administering of the magnetism to the 'victims', and the chaotic aftermath. Writing music like this, before the pictures even exist, is a totally different experience. With no narrative or visual clues, your imagination can run riot, but there's always the danger that you'll overcook the ideas and end up with something unworkable. Luckily, your music's played on the set, but is still not written in stone. Alterations can be made afterwards, before the final mix, as they were on this occasion.

The track played at the shoot was intended to inspire the participants to put as much excitement into the scene as possible. The final piece was less chaotic and clearer.

The Empty Room

The Body in Question was part of a canon of well-respected documentary series, and its thirteen hour long films had allowed us to explore the subject in depth. History and the arts had been used to tackle the science. Its presenter was such an engaging presence on screen that viewers were happy for him to take them on this in-depth investigation into their own form.

The thirteenth film was about death. The images are memorable, even now. Billowing curtains at an open window in a stark empty room; the deceased now an empty house where someone had once lived. To work on such a sombre subject could be difficult as a one-off programme, but as the conclusion to a thirteen-part series, it was the destination we'd all been working towards for well over a year.

There were difficulties along the way. Everybody on the team suffered a genuine crisis around programme eight. Programme eight's a very long way from the start, and yet painfully far from the finish. About Blood, it seemed to empty us all of every drop of creativity. I wondered if I could make it to the finish line, or whether I would become the body in question.

Starting work on programme nine put a spring back in our step. It's all in the mind, of course, but your energy levels and positive outlook are often under threat on such a long project, and it's such a relief when you feel you're on the home straight.

The Body in Question was an intense lesson in how to do the job.

Music for the series proved popular with the many people that worked on it. The title music and 'The Greenwich Chorus' had already been released as a single, but the director suggested that I produce a cassette of 'The Greatest Hits' to be distributed internally. So, having finished the series, I had time to take stock of all ninety minutes of material. It represented fourteen months of my time at the Workshop, and looking back on it now, charted a lot of my progress as a film composer.

The purchase of the polyphonic synth during my work on **The Body In Question**, and acquisitions for other composers, had made a whole host of new projects possible. We were now regarded, not only as a destination for special music and effects, but also fully fledged TV composers, competing with the best in the market. This was not what the original pioneers had envisaged, but for me nothing had been lost and a lot gained.

It was a rewarding time, knowing that there was a large appreciative audience out there. But I never imagined for a moment that I would play live to five and a half thousand of them twenty-nine years later.

The Doctor Who Prom

Blue Peter

We are playing at the Royal Albert Hall today, 13th July, 2013.

If the BBC National Orchestra of Wales had known about the abysmal standard of my sight reading, I'd have probably been barred from this whole escapade, but no, somehow I've slipped under the radar and in three days time, Mark Ayres and I are to play to a sell-out audience at the Albert Hall. Yes, we'll be a very small ingredient in a very big show, and yes we'll be tiny dots in the distance at the back of a giant orchestra, but we'll be playing a suite of classic **Doctor Who** pieces live to five and a half thousand people. Our section is part of a long programme of Murray Gold's music, wonderfully arranged by the conductor Ben Foster. Ben was one of my first students at the National Film and Television School[1]. Even then he was a much more able musician than me, but luckily was a great fan of vintage **Doctor Who**, and is clearly delighted to have Mark and I appearing on the bill.

We have had a couple of brief run-throughs with him at Maida Vale and

---
[1] I lectured on the Screen Music Course from 2003 to 2017

have duly arrived at the Albert Hall for the rehearsals two days before the concerts.

There's a lot more to the Albert Hall than meets the eye. To start with, there's a vehicle entrance on Prince Consort Road capable of taking an articulated lorry with no problem. It leads under the venue to a subterranean complex worthy of Doctor No. This houses dressing rooms and offices, as well as technical stores, common areas, and restaurants for the performers. In other words, back stage for the Albert Hall is really under the stage; under the whole arena. Lifts and stairs take you to the stage level, where you can walk out onto the rostra that support the players.

We've set up our gear at the back of the orchestra. I'm so close to the Henry Wood statue that I could reach out and touch it. Immediately to the other side of the statue is a mockup of the Doctor's TARDIS. In front of us, there sits the entire BBC National Orchestra of Wales. The horn section to the left, and down to our right, the largest percussion section I have ever seen.

Apparently, the rehearsal goes OK, although I feel very disconnected and 'out of the loop' stuck up here. It's like sending in a performance by carrier pigeon, compared with the instant feedback you get when performing in a studio. Of course, at the moment, the auditorium's empty apart from occasional crew; the vast numbers of us arranged on these steps seeming incongruous in the vast space.

We manage one run-through of the whole concert with the orchestra and have broken for lunch. During lunch, Mark and I end up chatting to Peter Davison in the artists' cafe, and around 2 o'clock we split up ready to re-convene at 3pm.

What I don't realise is that there's a crew from **Blue Peter** filming their presenter, Barney Harwood. He has rashly tried to learn the trombone in ten weeks so that he can play in the orchestra during the Prom. They want him to attend at least one rehearsal of the **Doctor Who** theme[2]. The trouble is they can't wait till 3 o'clock. The fervour with which some programme makers champion their own project is quite breathtaking. In their eyes, there's no mountain that can't be moved if their show demands it. Reschedule a full orchestra and chorus rehearsal in a tightly packed day full of artists, monsters and technicians, with all of them being informed of the change? No problem. So, suddenly, just after 2pm, there's a tannoy announcement that the rehearsal has been brought forward to 2.15pm, so that Barney Harwood can have a go at playing with an orchestra. The trouble is, there's no tannoy in the toilets, or at least not one that works. So I'm in there 'making the most of the break', when I get a text from Mark on my mobile[3].

"Where are you? We're all here, waiting on stage."

He was right. When I finally made it to the arena, the entire symphony orchestra was sitting there, waiting for me. It was a long climb up the rostra to my position at the back, made worse by the jeering and name calling from all the musicians. It was all in good humour, but it still felt like a public hanging.

The fact is, I've nothing against Barney Harwood for not being able to make the 3pm rehearsal; clearly, he had to be somewhere. The trouble is, so did I.

All the tribulations during rehearsals are instantly forgotten as soon as we get to the performance. The vast audience is laid out in front of me, over 270 degrees of vision. It's awe-inspiring. Children are on their fathers' shoulders, every single person excited and beaming from ear to ear. They are clearly here to enjoy themselves and that calms my nerves. I feel a small ingredient in a colossal event, one which is going to delight,

---

[2] Only reasonable, in the circumstances.
[3] Vodaphone clearly had no problem with reception in the toilets. Pity about the tannoy.

come what may. The complexity of this production's incredible. There are monsters and aliens all over the place. They've hired a choreographer to direct them. During rehearsals, she can be seen getting the Cybermen to descend the stairs down to the arena in formation. I'll hear later that during the performance one of the Cybermen falls over and loses his helmet. I seem to have that effect on Cybermen.

Our section goes OK. One of the most enjoyable moments for me was to play[4] the Horn of Rassilon on an Akai Wind Controller in that vast space. The sound was made from a re-pitched recording of the HMS Queen Mary siren. Somehow it seems very patriotic to play it in the Albert Hall.

The Doctor Who Prom is a vast exercise, meticulously organised and pre-arranged.

Such organisation would have seemed out of place in the early days, when we were just finding our feet.

My Doctor Who

It may come as something of a surprise, but the Radiophonic Workshop's involvement in the complete composition of incidental music for **Doctor Who** occurred many months before the title change was suggested. True, there were one or two musical contributions during the seventies. Malcolm Clarke had produced a real avant-garde electronic score for *The Sea Devils* in 1972, but its success didn't result in the Workshop being a regular musical contributor. I worked with Carey Blyton on the 1975 production, *Revenge of the Cybermen*. Again, a one-off job that wasn't the proper start of our self-penned scores for **Doctor Who.**

---

[4] Just two notes, actually two of the very few notes I had mastered. It was a new acquisition and I had only been playing it for a few days.

In the early seventies, Barry Letts had asked Brian Hodgson, who created sounds for **Doctor Who** at the time, whether the Workshop could make a greater contribution to the incidental music. Turning round such a high flow of work in a short time was more than the Workshop could handle at the time, and they put the idea on hold.

Much later, when the facilities improved, the idea resurfaced and, towards the end of 1979, John Nathan-Turner[5] talked to Brian about whether we could now deliver incidental music made entirely at the Workshop. To make sure that it was possible, they suggested Paddy Kingsland and I should produce a demo.

John sent across a mix of Episode One and Two of *The Horns of Nimon*, but without the music included. Over the next week, we tackled the score from the ground up using electronic sources[6]. **Doctor Who** post production schedules were notoriously tight, so we worked against the clock. The public never heard this early work; nor did other members of the Workshop.

To keep it under wraps, even the tape boxes had mock titles. The entry in the Radiophonic catalogue however is more forthcoming...

Composer	Peter Howell	TRW No.620
Title	Doctor Who Demo Tracks	
Series	Doctor Who	
Producer	John Nathan-Turner	
Department	Drama	
Requirement Service	BBC1	
Company Notes	Demo tracks for the 'Horns of Nimon'. Produced by Peter Howell as part of the proposal for the Workshop to take over providing all the series music in 1980.	

[5] Nathan-Turner had recently taken over as producer of **Doctor Who**.
[6] Paddy wrote music for Episode One and I scored Episode Two.

Clearly, this experiment was a success, and in due course, we were commissioned to write the incidental music for the upcoming season. By that time, I'd been asked to remake the title theme as well.

I assumed that Brian had asked all the composers whether they were interested; all I know is that he came to my studio one morning and said *"How do you feel about remaking Delia's* **Doctor Who** *theme?"*

There must have been a big pause. There was a lot going through my head, and it took a while.

"I'd love to try, but if it doesn't turn out OK, then I want to abandon it."

I was thinking of a failed update that had taken place a few years before. The result had reached a final programme, but was only broadcast in Australia (twice), before being pulled and never surfacing again. It was performed on the Workshop's favourite synthesiser of the time, the Synthi 100[7]. It was a great machine, but could not deliver the punch necessary for a theme of this sort. The sounds were wonderful, but on the thin side.

For that reason, I decided from the outset to use as many sound sources as possible. By the time I finished, I had used virtually everything in the Workshop, including the ARP Odyssey, EMS Vocoder, Yamaha CS80, Roland Jupiter, Synthi 100, tape manipulation, and many external boxes. I suppose there was another thing on my mind. Delia's version had taken the public by surprise and given them a really new audio experience, in the same way that the programme itself had taken the audience to new worlds and new times. I was excited to do the same. I wanted it to be unclear how it had been done. There were already a few synthesisers on the market and people were playing around, experimenting with them. I couldn't bear them chatting in the pub with their mates, telling them how

---

[7] Also known as 'The Delaware', named after Delaware Road where BBC Maida Vale was situated. For this reason, this version of the theme is known as the Delaware Theme amongst **Doctor Who** fans.

I had produced the theme. It would devalue it on the spot.

But what if it just didn't work?

If we decided that, after any amount of trying, it was a bad idea and should be abandoned, the one thing that concerned us was publicity. Not because we were frightened to fail, but because everyone would want to hear the failed attempt. It might even have more notoriety than a successful version. So, I had to work in secret.

So, with all these arrangements in place, work could begin.

Or thinking about work could begin.

The Steep Hill

The best place to start was the score.

Did Ron Grainer write anything down?

I asked in the Radiophonic office.

"Yes, of course, it's in the filing cabinet over there."

All that time, ever since I'd been at the Workshop, one of the most fascinating manuscripts had been within arm's reach. I was surprised it wasn't in a glass case somewhere.

I opened it on the desk. It was very slight; just the bare bones. There was the Dum dee Dum and the Ooo eee Ooo, the verse and the middle 8, but no harmonies were written out, just the occasional chord symbol.

I remember hearing an interview with Peter Sallis talking about his voicing of Wallace for the animation **Wallace and Gromit**. He remembers spending a whole day recording the dialogue for a film he had never seen, and at that time, a film that didn't exist. Animation is well known for being very slow and painstaking work, and he didn't hear back from Nick Park, the animator, for 18 months. When he did, it was an invitation to the screening. He was just blown away by the result.

"*Did I really do that?*" he said.

Word has it that Ron Grainer stood in the office before going on holiday, quickly jotting down his ideas for the **Doctor Who** title music on a single sheet of manuscript and dashing off for the plane.

When he came back to the Workshop many months later, he listened to Delia's creative rendition of his composition.

"My God, did I really write that?" he's reported to have said.

Delia had embellished his score in a way that nobody could have predicted, with a result that defied description. I can testify to that. I remember looking at the first episode of **Doctor Who** and listening to that music, and I couldn't describe it either.

This was a steep hill to climb. Could I make a version that could defy description? Well, no. However good it was, many years had passed since the first **Doctor Who**, and the public's perception of electro-acoustic music had moved on. Many of them could easily picture the sort of studio and equipment we used and were not easily blown away.

So, other objectives were necessary. Firstly, by using as many sorts of gear as possible, some mystique could be recreated. Secondly, because there was a vibrant music scene, it needed to interest this developing audience, as well as offering something fresh and interesting. If music engages your attention, you'll want to know what happens next.

In a way, this was one of the reasons that John Nathan-Turner had come to the Workshop. He wanted something arresting, but also contemporary. After all this time, it would be good to have it in stereo too.

One of the things discussed very early on, was the possibility of releasing a record (in those days a 45 rpm single) of the new theme. This was clearly an exciting prospect, but quite daunting for one important reason. If this was to be original and successful, it would feature some complicated procedures and recording techniques. In those days, repeating things was next to impossible, because there was no comprehensive way of remembering what you'd done. And yet, I was being asked to produce opening music, closing music and a record, which may have required me to repeat things three times. The way I solved this was to make the largest product first, the three minute record version, but embed the opening title music in the first forty-five seconds of it, and the closing in the final minute; the middle of this sandwich would have material just for the single release.

The idea proved to be a success, allowing me to concentrate on one pass of all the work.

Pitch Wars

I spent most of the first week trying ideas and sorting out the tempo and the key.

It's always a good idea to start work on a piece with something that's present most of the time. That way, you can establish a structure ready to support the other parts. Here the bass or 'Dum Dee Dum' was a constant thread.

I'd sorted out a sound on the CS80 that might provide the bulk of the bass sound. The lowest note in the original version of the theme had been a B, but the lowest B on the CS80 sounded too high[8]. The lowest note on the CS80 was C. So if the lead in note was C, then the key would have to be F minor.

How come the 1980 version of the theme is in F#m, then? I'm afraid that's due to a rather late decision. Having produced almost the whole three minutes of the record, I spent many sleepless nights worrying about the tempo. Did this sound contemporary enough or rather ploddy[9]?

The solution would involve a rather cumbersome process and that made me hesitate, but I eventually had to admit that it was too slow. In those days, you increased the tempo by altering the speed of the tape machine, and this would raise the pitch. If you just needed a slight increase, it would result in the pitch being somewhere between F and F#, and unplayable for conventional instruments, and a nightmare for whoever is writing the incidental music. So the choice was clear, it either had to be ploddy in F or contemporary in F#, nothing in between.

To this day, I still get complaints from weary composers thinking back to the 1980s and remembering how irritating it was to write the end cue of an episode so that it would lead naturally into the key of F#m. One small bonus with this speeding up, however, was that all the entries in the music were tighter and the overall feel slicker, which helped satisfy the brief.

We were eager for this to sound different from the very start and had originally worked on a mini sound sequence that was to occur before the first Dum dee Dum.

It was a long build up made from mixture of reversed bass notes and a gigantic flutter. This went up and down in pitch, finally to be lowered and slowed into the first bass note.

---

[8] What follows is not 'baffle-gab', to use a technical term. It does make sense, if anyone can be bothered to work it out!

[9] That is, with an overly slow and trudging beat

But when we put it with the visuals, it just seemed like such a long wait before we got going, and we dropped the idea in favour of the sting sound[10].

Dum Dee Dum

I needed to nail down the sound of the bass. The CS80 had a preset called 'Funk 1' and this was my starting point. This sound was too weak as single notes, but doubled in octaves sounded a lot thicker. Playing regular beats in the bass and adding the dotted (Dee) note only on the upper octave gave the part more depth and helped with the rhythm.

I'd sketched out the form of the piece as I've described, with the opening at the front, and the closing music at the end. I should mention that at this time there was not a real end, it just stopped. That was something that would have to be tackled later.

The climbing chords in the middle were yet to be thought of, and would cause some fuss and bother further down the line.

Anyway, I spent a day getting the bass part sorted by playing the CS80. I didn't use that instrument for anything else.

I'd decided that where possible I would deliver fresh sounds, without attempting to recreate any of Delia's ideas, but there was one sound she'd made that was just too good to ignore. This was the reverse gulp before each bass phrase. If we use the Dum Dee Dum language, I'm talking about something that you could describe as 'Er Dum Dee Dum'. It's easy to take for granted in her version, but it adds a lot of atmosphere. These lurching lead ups were indicated in Ron Grainer's original score, but he hadn't been specific about the sound.

---

[10] The sting was originally only on the front of the closing music. In fact, I used that original sound together with some newer ingredients on this new incarnation.

As you can hear, the reverse gulp sound only occurs before the first note of each phrase. Today, reversing audio is as easy as asking the computer to count from 10 to 1, rather than 1 to 10, but then it was a whole different matter. I was using a sixteen track Studer multitrack recorder at the time, which used two inch tape. If you wanted to have a sound on one of the tracks in reverse, you'd have to record it on track one, for example, and then turn the massive reel of tape over, and re-thread it into the machine. You then played the recording back, now in reverse, off track sixteen. But there was a further problem. The gulp sound had to precede each of those first notes, and it would be very hard to play half a beat early all the way through the piece.

I solved this by listening to the bass part in playback from the sixteen track machine and playing the first note of each phrase on the beat, but this time recording it onto a standard stereo machine. This was then easy to turn over and play in reverse, and play onto the multitrack ahead of the beat. Of course, you only had to get the first entry right and the whole piece would sync up. We'd all become adept at playing in tapes with split second accuracy[11], a skill that's been forgotten these days, and so I just had to start the new performance at the right place and record it back onto the multitrack with the rest of the bass part. Once it was correctly positioned, it gave the impression of tripping over, the feeling of being propelled forward.

There's a third ingredient to the bass sound. Reverse Reverberation. A strange effect, and one which can be heard in many feature films to this day.

I was using analogue tape machines, but the result can be achieved digitally today. First of all, I turned the large multitrack tape over, so that all the sounds were now playing backwards. I then played just the bass line into reverberation, with the reverb sound occurring after each note,

---

[11] There's a well known film of Delia Derbyshire showing off this skill, as she adjusts the synchronisation of one of three Philips tape machines by stopping and starting it whilst the other two machines are playing.

and recording it onto stereo tape. When you turn that recording over and play it the other way, the notes are playing forwards but the reverberation is playing backwards and precedes each note. This tape is then played back onto the multitrack, to sit alongside the original bass notes and the lurching lead up sounds.

The bass part of the **Doctor Who** theme is so important to the overall effect that I felt it was important to give it a unique sound.

Ooo Eee Ooo

Although it's the most remembered sound in the whole piece, the 'Ooo eee Ooo' is one of the easiest to reproduce and, odd though it may seem, was added to the track after a lot of the other ingredients. Nobody in their right mind would deliver a new version of the **Doctor Who** theme without that trade mark sound remaining pretty much the same, and so its the one sound that remains faithful to the original. When Delia produced it, she would have had to turn the knob on the front of the oscillator and perform the scoop sound that's so familiar. By the time I reproduced this, I used the portamento or glide on the ARP Odyssey.

Serpentine

For me, perhaps the most challenging and rewarding section to get right was the one that follows the first 'Ooo eee Ooo'. It steps down in four, three note phrases with some smaller passing notes. I'd already had a lot of experience with the EMS Vocoder in many programmes, but most extensively in **The Body in Question** for 'The Greenwich Chorus'. In that I'd managed to voice some quite meaningless, but interesting sounding phonetics to give the impression of a chorale. I was determined to have Vocoder featured somewhere in the **Doctor Who** theme, and started experimenting with these phrases. Whereas 'The Greenwich Chorus' had plenty of percussive consonants that made it rhythmically precise, the phrases I was dealing with here were totally unsuitable for consonants;

in fact it sounded rather stupid. What was needed was a long stream of vowels. Somewhere in storage, there still exists the multitrack of the piece featuring my embarrassing extended moans, shifting from one vowel to another, like a creature from another world. But when fed through the Vocoder and triggered by the notes of the tune, it takes on this shifting sound, and when mixed with the other ingredients of the track, seems to weave in and out, like something mercurial and difficult to pin down. To most people, these phrases will seem just part of the whole effect. The number of sounds playing at that moment means that simply playing the tune would get lost in the busy ensemble, but a sound that's serpentine and mysterious attracts our attention.

The Catherine Wheel

For a long while, there was a clip on YouTube of me giving a lecture about the making of the 1980 **Doctor Who** theme. I'm wearing a light blue jacket, looking rather young and very sure of myself. I can't remember doing this lecture at all, or where it might have been although I do remember the blue jacket. I was playing excerpts from the theme, and during the lecture I talked about the Catherine Wheel.

I had completely forgotten this in the intervening years, but apparently the sound that leads us out of the opening music, which as I've said occurs in the first 45 seconds of the record version, was modelled on the revolving sparks coming from a Catherine Wheel. This is one of two occasions in the theme where I was trying to achieve something so complicated, it demanded a concentrated period of work away from the main project.

Techniques in a studio around that time were holistic. The studio was brim full of gear, all dedicated to different functions, and the trick was to 'play' the whole room. To use the best of each bit of equipment as you needed, and to realise the result through recordings on the multitrack tape machine. It was often necessary to work on an individual idea that was to form part of the larger piece as a separate session, using a fresh lot of tape and treating it as a standalone job. Having mastered the sound on a quarter inch tape, you'd then play that back and record it onto a track of the main multitrack. So, here and there in the finished piece, ready made sequences would crop up.

The way the electronic sparks move was achieved in different passes. By the time this sequence had reached the final mix, it had been regenerated and augmented many times. White noise was quite appropriate here so the tape hiss caused by the copying just added to the effect.

The Catherine Wheel was one of those sub-jobs that seemed to take far longer than I hoped, but I was determined to see it through. There's always the possibility that it's a bad idea and will never get used, but until you've made it, you don't know whether it's good or bad. On this occasion it turned out OK and was added to the final mix.

So, how was the sound created?

I started with the recording of a match strike, where the initial percussive strike had been edited out, leaving the flare. I copied this many times and made a daisy chain of all the sounds, so it played as a tape loop. This still sounded too small and so I played it at half speed, resulting in something an octave lower and twice as slow. The resulting gaps between the sounds were filled by playing the loop through an echo machine set to the same speed, in order to provide a further iteration of the sound in every gap. To give it the feeling of movement, I introduced some phasing from a standalone phase unit. This complete assembly of sound was then re-recorded onto a new tape. In keeping with the lurching sounds elsewhere in the piece, I then 'hand spooled'[12] the tape and recorded it back onto the main multitrack of the theme music.

---

[12] This involved turning the right hand spool by hand, making the tape pass the playback head at a varying speed. Clearly, you'd have to have many attempts at this before it sounded right.

Balalaika

When Delia created the theme, everything was hard won. Each individual sound had to be made from very basic elements, often using a large oscillator and a lot of patience. This led to there being a smaller variety of sounds in any one piece. Apart from basic oscillators, a lot of sounds were garnered from actual recordings of live objects, which was a time-consuming process.

I was lucky enough to have a far greater choice of sounds at my disposal, and was determined to explore them as much as possible. However, anyone who has dabbled in such things will know that the sounds must still work together. If you can find a complementary sound that will act as a contrast to the rest then you're onto a winner.

So, when I started work on the middle eight bars of the theme, where the tune breaks away for a short while, I was rooting around for something surprising that would literally give us a break from the main section.

The middle eight in Ron Grainer's composition is a great moment. We've been in the moody depths of a minor key till now, and suddenly it's as if the sun has come out, everything is major chords, positive and promising. It's something that listeners look forward to, and it needs a bright inviting sound.

I set out around the studios to try and find the ideal sound. I settled on a Roland Jupiter in Paddy Kingsland's studio. Many synthesisers of that period featured an arpeggiator. When you held down a chord, it would automatically play each note of the chord in quick succession. You could also ask it to travel over 1, 2, or 3 octaves, whilst playing the same notes in each octave. I thought it might be interesting to hear the tune of the middle eight hidden amongst arpeggios, running up and down. A sort of encoded variation of the tune. That didn't work and was far too confused. However, if you selected two octaves but just pressed a single note, then the machine would assume that you wanted that note from each octave and would oscillate from one to the other very fast. It gave an interesting glassy tremolo, like an electronic mandolin or balalaika. I settled on this. We visit this alternative sound world for a short while, long enough to make our return to the main theme a sort of homecoming.

I decided that it was easier to leave the Roland synthesiser in Paddy's studio, and use his multitrack to make the recording, so fetched the two inch tape and laid down a take or two.

It was only after I'd done that and heard the rest of the theme, that I decided to move into the middle eight through a haze of shifting sounds, and after it to slide the end note downwards and fade it out. This seemed to me almost like a passing comet that comes into view, dazzles for a while and then disappears into the depths of space. All this required another visit to Paddy's studio later in the process, to work on those additional ideas. In fact, I was to go back there a third time, right at the end, to do the final mix.

There were a few bars in my arrangement that were not Grainer, but Howell! The rising chords before the final push in the record version were intended as a relief from the pattern of tune and middle eights that had preceded them. Over the length of a record, this would have become too predictable. The sound's very simple, the trombone stop on the Roland Jupiter. You could say it's a palate cleanser ahead of the final headlong descent into the end sequence, and that final explosion.

Serendipity

The happy accident or serendipity has always been a good friend to the artist. It's only the pretentious few who would try to suggest that every single thing has been painstakingly thought through.

What happens at the end of the 1980 theme is the result of the most bizarre coincidence, caused by a rather arcane piece of BBC engineering protocol.

For many years, BBC engineering had insisted that tapes were stored 'end out', because of something called 'print through'. When a very sudden and loud sound was recorded it would cause such a disturbance in the magnetic layer on the tape that it would print through to the next layer, and play back quietly one revolution later. It's similar to the indentations left on a sheet of paper from the writing on the sheet above. The effect was most pronounced if the recording was followed by silence, when the echo could be easily heard. To avoid this, the engineers insisted that after a recording, the tape was spooled further forwards so that the whole reel ended up on the right-hand spool. There was leader tape (coloured tape with no recording surface) at the end of each reel, so it was easy to see if a spool had been left end out. The tapes used on multitracks were expensive, and so any unwanted spools were re-used.

There was a cupboard under the Synthi 100. To be honest, there were a lot of empty spaces in the Synthi 100, including the space behind a knob labelled 'Option 4' which was not attached to anything, but proved invaluable if a director wanted 'hands on' involvement in the production of the piece. Anyway, the large cupboard which extended along the whole length of the synthesiser, ended up being stuffed full of used tapes from Dudley Simpson's **Doctor Who** music sessions.

Dudley, who composed the music for the series from 1964 to 1980, used live players to form the bulk of his incidental music and then brought the multitrack tape of that recording up to the Workshop, where electronic music was added. Since the great majority of this music would be produced on the Synthi 100, it was only natural that the discarded tapes found their way into this cupboard.

I'd pulled one of these out to use, when I first started work on the 1980 theme. It had been left 'end out'. In order to listen to the recording on it, therefore, you'd have to fast wind through the whole reel back to the beginning.

None of us at the Workshop particularly held to this protocol of 'end out' storage, and would often use the tape from the end to the beginning. After all, the iron filings which formed the surface of the magnetic tape didn't care which way they were going.

So, in order to make sure that the tape I was using was free of any previous recordings, I erased three minutes of it. A record version of the theme was highly unlikely to be longer than three minutes, so this seemed more than enough.

It was several weeks of hard work before I reached what was to be the end of the piece, and I'd long since forgotten that the tape I was using had previously been used. Because of a longer amount of run up time on the front, and the piece generally being longer than I expected, I was unwittingly close to the end of the erased section. In fact, by complete chance, this boundary between erased and unerased tape occurred just after the last note of the theme. As I laid down the final note, strange sounds started to play back. Not only strange, but surprisingly effective sounds. It took me by surprise.

In fact, the percussion recording from one of Dudley Simpson's sessions had started to play, and because the tape had been stored end out, these percussion sounds were playing backwards. As many of you will know, recordings of instruments like cymbals sound very odd and eerie when played backwards, and that was what was happening here.

Until that moment of serendipity, I'd never thought of having a short sound sequence at the end of the theme. Such happy accidents should never be wasted, and I set about seeing how such a sequence of sounds could lead us to some sort of big finish. At this point I reached for something that had been discarded right at the beginning. The background wash that was originally intended to open the piece. The one that we'd dropped in favour of the sting. That, together with a reprise of the Catherine Wheel, and some reverse percussion from the Dudley Simpson session, made up this sound designed tail.

So that leaves just one more thing. The explosion.

Whiteout

Explosions are easy on a synthesiser. White Noise generators with a sharp attack on the envelope give a fairly instant result, but it often lacks punch and can sound rather generic and like any other explosion. So, I looked round for a way to inject some originality into it. It was a long search.

Eventually, I discovered a cupboard full of discarded gear. These were various effects boxes that were no longer used, or had ceased to work properly, and given their age and lack of use, were not worth resuscitating. In amongst these cast-offs was a small box about the size of a bag of sugar. The Countryman Phaser. This acquisition had never been a success. Phasing had become popular in some early pop records. The drum break effects on the song 'Itchicoo Park' were made by recording a sound over two reel-to-reel tape machines, and microscopically altering the distance between the record and playback heads on one machine. Perhaps that's a discussion for another day, but they used a pencil to achieve it!

Quite a palaver. Imagine the delight when electronic alternatives to this process became available. The Countryman Phaser was one of them, but it had one major problem. It only used batteries, and they ran out ridiculously quickly. As the power drained, the sound became choppy and distorted. Over time, this was the only sound that the device would make, even with new batteries; an ideal choice for dirtying up the end explosion. I'd set out to use as much of the gear at the Workshop as possible, and now it even included broken stuff as well.

Throughout my work on the theme, I'd been collaborating with a graphic designer, Sid Sutton. Although I was engaged in making a record version at length, the main reason I was doing it at all was to accompany the opening and closing titles of the programmes.

Sid and I had several initial meetings and discussed the idea of the moving star field. He was intending to layer the stars so that they shifted differently according to their distance. Such effects were harder to achieve back then, and the result was regarded as highly innovative.

Once I'd settled on how the piece would finish, I phoned Sid up to talk about the end explosion. He was surprisingly cautious, especially about the idea of having a whiteout.

Apparently, in the days of film, one of the worst things you can do is have frames of total white. The reason is simple, dirt. The tiniest scrap of dust or worse will be magnified and look terrible. There was even some official engineering edict to that effect, and so Sid would have had his work cut out to persuade them to accept it. As anyone can see, it did pass the censors, and even if the white wasn't pure as driven snow, the effect makes the end of the credits something special.

These days, that explosion's also the last sound in our concerts.

Remaking the title music for **Doctor Who** was a wonderful experience. I had plenty of time, plenty of resources, and crucially a lot of support from the other members of the department. Their reaction to the various elements of the piece, as they gradually came into being, was so important. I was being allowed to rebuild a piece of music that had become iconic, and the reaction of the audience would make or break it.

Entering the TARDIS

Around that time, **Doctor Who** took over my working life. The title music was barely coming to an end, when I received the first viewing tapes of *The Leisure Hive*. It was time to revisit my early attempts at incidental music, in those demos with Paddy Kingsland, and remind myself of what we'd promised. Time to enter the TARDIS.

Writing incidental music for **Doctor Who** was most certainly bigger on the inside.

It was a place where time contracted, where you needed to be in two places at once, and where just when you thought you had finished, everything started all over again.

What struck me first was how many trees were involved.

As soon as you were on the team, a fat pile of pink sheets would appear in your in-tray. The Shooting Script.

And, a week or so later, another pile, this time yellow. The Edit Script.

TV and film scripts are spaced out to allow more room for notes and additions, and to make them easier to read, so only the centre of the page is used. All the lines are double spaced, so very little's achieved in one single sided page.

It's hard not to regret **Doctor Who**'s contribution to climate change, especially because I never read one page of these paper mountains. If lines and scenes were ditched in the edit, why waste time imagining what music you would have written, what really mattered was the final programme. Everything else was irrelevant.

In fact, your first meeting with the director was to look at the edit of an episode. And so it was with the first episode of my first **Doctor Who** adventure.

Advertising	November 1979	TV Schools	BBC1
Quest	November 1979	TV Bristol	Regional TV
Doctor Who Signature Tune Remake	November 1979	Drama	BBC1
Spotlight	January 1980	Plymouth	Regional TV
Escape	January 1980	General Features	BBC2
Doctor Who (5N): The Leisure Hive	January 1980	Drama	BBC1 Incidental Music

The director, Lovatt Bickford, had a very particular style. Not only did he record the video action using a method more akin to feature films than television[13], but his requirements from me were equally grandiose. After our first meeting, I got the impression that he wanted music everywhere, and for it to be as large a scale as possible.

I naively agreed, and in fact was excited to be asked. Looking back, I think he and I were in cahoots over this. We both saw the opportunity to deliver something special in the first adventure of a revamped series, and were determined to give the audience a memorable experience.

However, neither the budget nor the shooting timescale were large enough for our aspirations. Frequently, I had to make up for visuals that had been hurriedly put together, giving them a score they didn't deserve. Grand and portentous music over an ineffective shot will emphasise its deficiencies.

---

[13] One camera is used in films, and the scenes acted several times for different camera angles. In TV, the action takes place once and will be captured by several cameras.

For example, there was a closeup of the rockets firing on a space shuttle as it came ever closer to landing. The shot took forever. One way of making everything seem more important on a low budget film is to hold the shots for longer, but this one lingered and lingered. And then lingered some more. The Special Effects had done a sterling job in making the shuttle, but I don't think they were expecting the shot to last as long.

Dick Mills, who was contributing sound FX for this sequence, agreed. He had already described it as 'the very slow approach of poached eggs', and spent about ten minutes producing the necessary whoosh, and left the rest to me. It was my job to lift this out of the culinary into the stellar. I'd done something similar for that steak and kidney pie earlier in my career, so they had come to the right person.

I remember toiling over this cue. Out of all my music for **Doctor Who**, *The Leisure Hive* draws on more classical references than any other. Faced with the daunting task of supplying feature film music, it's not surprising that I resorted to the same influences as countless other movie composers. Wagner, Stravinsky, and Holst must have been revolving in their graves at a steady 15 inches per second on hearing *The Leisure Hive*. They were joined in Episode 4 by Ravel; the repetitive nature of his Bolero seemed too good to miss during the Doctor's brush with the human photo-copier.

The irony of my situation was that I was trying to recreate orchestral sized sounds in a room almost within touching distance of the back wall of Studio MV1, where virtually every day of the week a full orchestra was doing just that. It was a wonderful challenge, and I enjoyed it, but for me I think scores for other **Doctor Who** adventures, such as *Meglos* and *The Five Doctors*, are more innovative and could be described as electronic music.

Not all the music for *The Leisure Hive* could be so easily dismissed as the Shuttle Arrival. I think the cue between Brighton Beach and Argolis is one of my best incidental cues for **Doctor Who**, and I remember being in the studio working on it. I've mentioned that the goal in an electronic studio at that time was to source sound from across the studio. This is something that I've carried on to this day; cherry picking sounds and getting them each to do what they are good at. If the musical narrative's always changing, it keeps you guessing; you're interested to hear where it goes next.

The deadlines for *The Leisure Hive* were relaxed to start with, but similar to all subsequent adventures, the closer you got to the final episode, the tighter the time. This concertina effect was so marked that the window of work would shrink from ten to six days. Schedules were broken, the studio a mess, and energy in short supply. You vowed to be more organised next time.

Meglos

Technology Programme	March 1980	Finnish Service	External Services
Doctor Who 5Q: Meglos	April 1980	Drama	BBC1 Incidental Music

John Nathan-Turner and I felt, in retrospect, that the music could have had a more accompanying role in the first adventure.

My second one, *Meglos*, would allow me to do just that.

It was full of hooded figures and ceremony, so I used the vocoder to make a chorus of chanting electronic priests. These clearly inspired Douglas Adams when he created his Electric Monk in *Dirk Gently's Holistic Detective Agency!*[14]

---

[14] You and I know that is completely untrue!

I must have decided all that from my sick bed[15], because Paddy Kingsland composed the music for Episode 1, and I dealt with 2, 3, and 4. Composing's a rather self-centred activity, and handing over the reins to someone else is a challenge. Even in more predictable orchestral scoring, it's hard for the newcomer to imitate another's style, but in the idiosyncratic world of electronic music it can never be done seamlessly. The approach is never the same, and there's no convenient written score.

Also, imagine how daunting it would be to re-create sounds that another person had made, when the equipment didn't memorise anything. So, when I took over from Paddy, I continued the score as I would have done if I'd been well. He and I were very aware of the differences in our styles, but it was less of a problem for the viewers.

The pictures lead the ideas when you write incidental music, so when faced with the good Doctor breaking out in a skin condition resembling a cactus, a vibraslap[16] was the sound that immediately sprang to mind. This rattlesnake-like resonator has what can only be described as a prickly sound. I'm sure that many composers have similar traits, but in electronic music where the sounds are so varied, it's useful to pin them down in your mind with an association, even if it's visual.

But the most memorable piece of music in *Meglos* wasn't in the final mix at all.

There's a sequence (I think it's in Episode 2) when the Meglos version of the Doctor apprehends Caris and they march off the set holding on to one another. To me it just looked as if they were dancing the tango. So I wrote an arrangement of 'Hernando's Hideaway' and threw it over the action. It worked uncannily well; to modern audiences it would look like a scene out of *Strictly Come Dancing*. I never intended to use it, but we

---

[15] For years, I was convinced it had been Paddy who had gone sick and I had taken over from him, but I'm reliably informed that I was the sick one.
[16] A large U-shaped spring that has a wooden bell containing a striker on one end and a surface to hit at the other.

could all have a good laugh at the final mix and then replace it with the proper music. Unfortunately, John Nathan-Turner didn't notice there was anything wrong. Everyone in the room looked in his direction, primed to share the joke... nothing happened. In fact, we ploughed on to the end of the mix, but were then faced with a difficult situation. We couldn't let the programme go out with someone else's tango stuck in the middle of it. We'd have to draw attention to the producer's lack of observation. Which is what we did. Not only did the joke fall flat, but we spent the rest of the session wondering whether JNT was irritated or embarrassed[17].

It was a trivial event, but it does highlight how vulnerable you can suddenly be. We all go through life imagining there are checks and balances in place, that being further down the food chain, we are not exposed to the risks that our superiors have to face. But what if those checks don't operate?

Many years later, I wrote music for a splendid drama called *Life Story*[18] about the discovery of DNA, and in amongst my original music had been a cover version of a Georges Delerue piece as we moved around the giant model of the double helix. The film's paperwork had made it clear that I was not the composer, but the end credits on the film did not[19]. Months after it had gone out, I received a phone call from New York, patched through to my studio in Maida Vale. It was Georges Delerue's agent complaining that I'd received the credit for his client's work. The matter was easily resolved, but I suddenly felt very exposed.

It's easy to forget that working in a studio in Maida Vale is not as solitary as it might seem. Material that will only be heard in your presence by a few individuals, will be experienced by millions, but things like that seem rather irrelevant when you're struggling to get your music to fit the picture.

---

[17] Probably neither.
[18] A **Horizon** special, first shown on BBC2 on 27 April, 1987.
[19] My credit had read 'Music by', when it should have read 'Original Music by', indicating that there had been work by other composers.

Because of its connection with **Doctor Who**, the Workshop was often viewed as a TV department, but it wasn't. It had been radio's need for special sound that had kick started the Workshop. Television jumped on the bandwagon, and we were excited that it had, but none of us received any advice or guidance about working with visuals. Perhaps we were regarded as such mavericks that any conventional suggestions were unlikely to apply, but that was very far from the truth.

We still had to get our heads round how to use all this film and video gear. To figure out how music and sound related to pictures. How it would embed itself in the scenes. We really were flying solo. When something worked, it would affect how you'd tackle further projects, but it was a 'suck it and see' approach.

There was another drag on our productivity; the laborious matching of music to picture.

For us, synchronisation was never easy. There was no computer to do all the maths for you, and so it was always tricky to stitch the music and picture together.

We were forced to work with a primitive video cassette machine to view the pictures. It would look like a period piece today. This self-contained unit with its own small screen was originally intended for commercial, industrial, or medical uses. It had no means of communicating with any other device. Once loaded, the videotape, which was in black and white, would pass over a helical scan head, but in every other regard it was just like an audio reel-to-reel tape recorder. The controls were woolly and imprecise. All right for viewing a whole tape at a time, but not suited to the constant playing, stopping. and rewinding that was necessary when preparing and scoring.

Perhaps it comes as a surprise to learn that the Workshop took decades to become 'state-of-the art'. We lagged behind other parts of the BBC and most of the industry for many years. Our department had always been a dumping ground for gear that no one else wanted. It was that 'magic attic' vibe that attracted people in the days of Daphne Oram and Delia Derbyshire, and continued to do so in the late seventies. But this quirky image was less welcome to those of us trying to deliver too much music in too little time. Working with an old video machine was frustrating when you knew that Television Centre was locking picture to sound every day. But then, requesting picture syncing gear from radio would have simply raised eyebrows, so some ad-hoc negotiations with TV were necessary to get even these basic machines.

With no way of locking the pictures to the sound, we all had to find our own ways of getting round the problem of synchronisation.

Mine was old school and elicited many snide comments from my colleagues. I made a recording of my voice dictating every second and minute for over an hour, whilst looking at a stopwatch[20]. Whenever I started a new multitrack tape, I copied this time recital onto track eight. Listening to this, I'd know the relationship between that instant and the timecode in vision. Of course there was a problem with this system. Imagine listening to a voice rhythmically reciting numbers, one every second, and trying to play a line of music at a different tempo; it would be like tapping your head and rubbing your stomach. So I used to look at a point on the video of **Doctor Who** and make a note of the timecode.

Finding the exact point on the tape using my spoken timings, I'd mark the recording tape with a thick vertical line, and pull the tape back from right to left, keeping the chinagraph[21] on the tape and drawing a wavy line. That way, I'd constructed a visual cue, and didn't need to listen to the spoken track. Now, I could play the instrumental line and make sure

---

[20] BBC Stopwatches were heavy and very solid. I remember one hapless Studio Manager telling us of the time he had run for a bus down Regent Street, having forgotten that he had his stopwatch in the pocket of his plastic mac. He missed the bus, doubled up on the pavement.
[21] This is a wax crayon.

I coincided a certain point (a chord, for instance) with the vertical line.

Heath Robinson would have been proud.

Warriors' Gate

Rumpole	May 1980	Drama	Radio 4
Kid Jensen Holiday Special	May 1980	Radio 1	Radio 1
Doctor Who Theme Record (RESL 80)	June 1980	BBC Enterprises	BBC Records
Turning Point	July 1980	TV Science Features	BBC2
Doctor Who (Serial 5S): Warriors' Gate (Music)	August 1980	Drama	BBC1 Incidental Music

I'm always drawn to those adventures that contain featured cues, when the music's accompanying a particular event at some length.

We were always poking fun at the amount of 'corridor creeping' that happened in **Doctor Who** adventures. Sometimes, in order to make the corridor look longer, they would cut halfway through to a shot of the characters walking back down the same corridor, but without seeing them turn round, they would seem to be walking further. I'm glad to say *Warriors' Gate* didn't suffer from corridor creeping and instead contained a few scenes with featured music. There was the banqueting music and the Versailles-like scene in the garden, as well as the waking of the Tharils. A welcome opportunity to write a score that was more standalone. The Gundan robots also gave me a chance to come out of my musical shell, even if the bass interval was rather reminiscent of Prokofiev's 'March' from *Romeo and Juliet*.

From a musical perspective, this story was a welcome change for me. We were joining a world that had a sense of the unknown and of mystery, where things happened according to laws that we would never understand. Music's good at alluding to things we can't see, adding extra pieces to a puzzle.

I allowed myself some licence on the garden scene, and wrote everything in a whole tone scale, reminiscent of Debussy. I remember being fascinated by his music when I was younger. There's something refreshing and unusual about it, as if it's only just rained and everything's washed clean. Musicians are playing in an adjoining room in the banqueting scene. These days adding such an acoustic would be easy. There are so many software solutions, but at the time choices were limited.

When I joined the Workshop, there was an echo room built specially for us which used a compact room at the bottom of the stairs leading to the studios in the basement. It was about twelve feet long, and six feet across, with plastered walls and ceiling. Down one end there was a speaker[22], and down the other end a microphone. Upstairs in each Radiophonic studio, amongst the myriad of ins and outs on the jack field[23] you'd find 'Echo Room In' and 'Echo Room Out'. There was nothing to stop more than one studio using the facility, but like a party line on the old GPO telephones, if you heard other people's material coming back through the 'Echo Room Out' socket, you knew it was in use.

I'd decided not to use any of the echoes on offer for the banqueting music. Something customised was called for.

There was a favourite technique used in BBC drama, known as Acoustic

---

[22] Just one. This was mono.
[23] A jack field is a strip (or many strips) of sockets, allowing you to cross plug audio ins and outs.

Effects Reproduction or AER. The technique's still in use today and is called 'Worldising', a clumsy 'Hollywood' term, but it involves a very similar process. It involves playing your sound into a real acoustic, and re-recording it onto a new tape. It's very much affected by where you place the microphone to re-record. The further away from the speaker, then the more of the room is added. There was an acoustic that was ready made for the Banqueting music; the void behind my studio in the bowels of BBC Maida Vale. Where the lower corridor ran beside the studio walls, there was all the reflective stonework and distance needed to sound like a echoing castle. I would have to choose an evening when there were no bookings in the orchestral studios. The spaces between the studios were there to control the sound pollution between one studio and another, and it wouldn't have been popular for me to be doing this during the day. To get the sound to and from the void, I'd need a couple of long cables.

These were stored in a cupboard at the end of a narrow room further up the long corridor. I thought everyone had gone home for the night, and that it was just me and the commissionaire. I stepped into the room. The lighting was bright around the door, but blue and very dim elsewhere. As I looked into the gloom, I saw six boxes, coffin shaped but taller. From the middle of them, a strange wailing voice arose. I knew what these strange boxes were, but the sound made me shiver nonetheless. Clearly, someone else was working late.

When the rock music studios were built downstairs, they installed echo plates; well away from the studios, to make sure there was no interference with the recordings. They were basic in design: a metal sheet suspended in a long box with a transducer[24] on one end and a pickup on the other. More hi-tech than the echo room, it had the advantage of a dedicated echo plate for each studio. Audio was played at one end of the metal plate and picked up at the other. I was hearing a female singer in Studio MV4 being echoed along the plate. No doubt it was one of the Peel Sessions which were often being recorded in MV4 and MV5.

---

[24] A device that converts audio into vibrations that simulate a loudspeaker.

I retrieved the cables I needed and walked back to my studio.

These excursions around the building were often part of work on a special cue. If a piece of music had particular requirements, as in the Banqueting music for *Warriors' Gate*, then it could take many hours, and the other cues got squeezed.

Having finished work on an episode, we would travel to Television Centre in Shepherd's Bush, to mix the music with the other sounds and dialogue. This final mix or dub took a whole day.

These dubs took place in the Cypher Suite. It was state-of-the-art and had the ability to keep an eight track tape in sync with the master video of the programme. The ingredients of the show, dialogue, sound effects and music played back from tracks one to four, and the final mix was recorded onto five and six. Track eight carried timecode which locked the whole thing together, and track seven was used for any extras. There was a serious lack of track space, and not much opportunity to be that creative, so Dick Mills' sounds and my music had to be completely finished and ready to go as soon as we'd transferred them from our tapes to the multitrack.

A few things are memorable from these sessions, and not all of them relate to the music. Ever since attending film dubs, I've come to the realisation that of all the times you're most likely to catch the flu, the day after a dub is favourite. It's a perfect storm. Not only have you probably worked through the night to finish the music, but because of your 'visitor' status at the dub you'll most likely be sitting on the sofa at the back of the dubbing theatre; the clothes you're wearing will be the same clothes that you went to work in the day before, when it was sunny and rather warm. In order not to interfere with the sound from the studio speakers, the air conditioner will always be positioned at the back of the dubbing theatre above your head and because the gear in the studio will give out a fair amount of heat, it'll be set to cold. There can be only one outcome:

the flu.

Not known for my forward planning, I've at least got used to preparing for dubs these days and turn up ready for anything.

From a more technical point of view, one issue would dominate; the sonic argument between the sounds and the music. **Doctor Who** featured special sound effects from the days of William Hartnell, the first Doctor. Some of them had noticeable pitches, low drone notes that would make adding music a challenge. It had not been a problem when they were first conceived; there might not have been any music. But during similar scenes in later adventures, that original sound and any new music would have to coexist[25]. Both have a right to be there, but something has to give. The **Star Wars** movies were well under way by then, the first in 1977 and *The Empire Strikes Back* in 1980. Anybody listening to the fabulous soundtracks of either of those films will be struck by the clarity of each scene. Most of the time, they've taken a decision; either the music or the sounds have precedence. When the music leads, there are few sounds and almost always no background sound at all. No equipment hum, room tone or even outside atmosphere. They took the view that though it might be counter intuitive to 'turn off' the atmosphere when the music's playing, it just works better if you do. In **Doctor Who** dubs, it was almost impossible to persuade a dubbing mixer to take out the background sounds under the music. He felt a sort of obligation to present the world the way it was[26], without any high handed decisions to change it.

But whatever my reservations about the soundtrack, the adventures we mixed in that dubbing suite between 1980 and 1984 were well received and a large fan base still searches them out on Amazon to this day.

---

[25] From 1980, when the workshop provided sounds and music, there could be more collaboration between the two.
[26] To distort reality ran counter to the old BBC imperative, and it was still alive and well in scifi drama which of course was not about the real world anyway.

K9 and Company

I have always been enthusiastic to try something new. The results are often exciting, but not always successful. But I think my interest in new challenges was sometimes misinterpreted, because I was the first person asked to score anything that went out once and took an age to work on. It was a trend I found hard to break[27]. It resulted in long hours spent on short straws. Every year, for instance, the BBC would make a one-off programme about itself. It was a documentary about how much the licence payers were getting for their money. A suitably grand opening theme was required, but with no money for live musicians.

Not all the one-offs were so gruelling; some were great fun, although destined to fail.

I was responsible for the music on **K9 and Company**, a pilot featuring **Doctor Who**'s metal hound and the wonderful Elisabeth Sladen[28] as Sarah Jane. Ian Levine wrote the titles as an orchestral score, but John Nathan-Turner asked me to do an electronic version.

This was the age of new synthesisers, and everyone was eager to use them. Our combined enthusiasm resulted in the eighties synth boom and some painfully cliched pieces of music. They still litter movies of the period; some of them, great films that were marred by their scores.

You might find my version of Ian's music on YouTube.

I can't take all the blame. The opening visuals were atrocious. The first picture of Elisabeth Sladen is so long it becomes a static portrait; no doubt waiting for the shot of K9 which had to sync with the beat.

Comments on the site say it all…

---

[27] I'm glad to say that once the nineties were upon us, it was no longer cost effective.
[28] She was not only loved by the fans but also by those who worked with her. Her early death was a terrible blow to us all.

'The opening's just gloriously awful. I adore it.'

'So eighties, it's painful.'

You get the idea.

Because of the sudden ease with which we could make this kind of music, I would be only too pleased to churn out these synth celebrations at a moment's notice. I'm glad to say that they only represented a tiny part of my output of that period and have been binned along with the haircut and the flared trousers.

Kinda

We took on stories in rotation, and my turn had come round again.

Kinda is popular with many fans, but I found it hard. I must have been at a low point creatively, having had over two years of constant activity; the incidental experiments, a new arrangement of the title music, three **Doctor Who** adventures to score (*The Leisure Hive*, *Meglos*, and *Warriors' Gate*), and the normal batch of material for other BBC programmes. In addition, when I first viewed *Kinda*[29], I was very disappointed in its studio bound appearance. All the adventures I'd done to date had a very particular feel and were atmospheric pieces, especially *Warriors' Gate* which preceded it. But this one seemed to be an exercise in shadowless lighting[30]. We are in a colonial outpost in the middle of a jungle, with very few windows, and yet there's not a dark corner. Outside, even though we are in the forest, we just seem to be over the other side of the same studio. In fact, I know that all that vegetation was standing in pots on the studio floor, and when we were supposed to be further into the forest,

---

[29] The name's rather disappointing as well. You can't even Google it without getting 'We got a groovy kinda love'!

[30] I had worked in lighting at Glyndebourne Festival Opera many years before, and achieving such an overall bright light without shadows is clever. For the BBC though, it was more to do with catering for poor TV reception.

they moved the same pots round to form another set. What you saw is what you got. All the more reason to ask for atmospheric lighting to give it some depth.

I may be accused here of exceeding my brief, it may seem inappropriate for a composer to talk about lighting, but it's important. Right from my first experience of writing applied music, the other ingredients in the production have always influenced me. They are the catalyst for the composition, so the relentlessly bright visuals might have contributed to the bland score.

There's far too much of the same synthesiser[31] in this, symptoms perhaps of a punishing schedule. I relieve this synth tedium on occasions by the use of sampled audio. A bowed cymbal sound for the snake tattoo, and some flanged glass sounds for the hanging chimes. I lifted those glass sounds from the collapse of the witch's glasshouse, something I did when I first joined the Workshop. It always pays to keep a good database of previous assembly material when deadlines are tight!

The criteria you use to judge your own work is often at odds with other people's expectations. After all, if the music moves the narrative along and doesn't get in the way, it's indulgent to expect it to do otherwise. Somehow though, we were always aware of where we were, and what the Department had achieved to date. It had built a reputation on innovative sound and music, and it's a pity if time or tiredness prevented you from breaking new ground.

Snakedance

I'd never heard of a Janissary Band prior to working on the **Doctor Who** adventure *Snakedance*[32]. It refers to a style of playing from the Turkish

---

[31] The CS80 had been my favourite synthesiser for many years, but whenever you use too much of one sound source in any score it can become predictable and unexciting.

[32] *Snakedance*, the sequel to *Kinda*, was a TV debut for Martin Clunes, who has done his best to avoid wearing a skirt ever since.

Ottoman Empire, and features loud drums and bells, together with some very brash brass. The Janissary Band's an exuberant sound that seems to ignore the sanctimonious attitude of a lot of Western classical music. If its players feel the slightest misgivings about the strident noise they're making, then they would all have to pack up and go home. It's their confident performance that gives the music its vitality. I remember having a ball re-creating the Janissary Band on the Fairlight's composer page. This was my first outing with the new computer driven synth. It greatly increased our choice of sounds.

It wasn't only new technology that had improved the workflow. I'd developed better ways of working and was producing over two minutes of sync'd music a day[33].

The need to write, perform and record music in a short timescale would always be a challenge, but with such a high demand for music, there was no time to worry about 'Writer's Block'[34]. Getting something recorded was key. It didn't matter what it was. After all, 'being bad and making good' is the best way to deliver.

I used a few tricks to ensure that first idea was easier to come by.

The 'Washing Line' technique, for example.

A single high string line was recorded throughout the length of the piece. This would act as a reference point, allowing phrases or chords to be literally hung on the washing line. Even if the held string note disappeared as the ideas progressed, it had got me off the starting blocks.

Or the 'Destinations' technique, where rather than pinpointing every event in a scene, a destination point could serve as a target. A more coherent piece could be written in a shorter time without the distraction

---

[33] This is from the first moment I saw the scene, to the finished music ready for broadcast.
[34] The idea that your creative juices dry up and you stare at a blank page.

of the intermittent sync points.

Whatever technique you used, you'd started. Improving or re-imagining it would always be relative to that initial act of creation, and easier to accomplish. As Daniel Barenboim remarked in a talk about sound and silence, once we've broken the silence nothing is the same again[35]. All subsequent sounds will relate to that first note, and the music will determine its own content.

Showing Up

There was a steady trickle of **Doctor Who**-related events that demanded our attention, and despite ongoing work we were only too pleased to attend. My first experience of a convention was at the Hilton Hotel. It was in Edgware Road and only about a mile from BBC Maida Vale, so it was an easy invitation to accept.

Dick had warned me it would be "quite full on", but the scale of it surprised me; I signed so many autographs on that day that I even forgot my own name. Gazing at one fan's badge, I wrote his name instead of my own.

The Hilton Hotel had reserved two floors for the event which must have seemed perfectly reasonable at the planning stage, and indeed the planned events did fit into those two floors well. What they hadn't bargained for was the transit of fans through the foyer and up in the lifts.

I was first struck by the Ice Warrior asking directions at the reception desk and then there appeared to be a Silurian sitting at a table reading a newspaper. I crossed the lobby through a mixture of fans and hotel guests and entered the lift. A woman with her suitcase was already in it, and a Sontaran. He seemed very big and didn't say anything, which only made the woman more nervous.

---

[35] See his article 'The Phenomenon of Sound' for more detail. (https://danielbarenboim.com/the-phenomenon-of-sound/)

I'm not sure, but I can't help feeling that it was the first and last **Doctor Who** event hosted by the Hilton Edgware Road.

We are still asked to appear at signing days. Often very well run and enjoyable to do.

On one occasion, at an appearance of a different sort, it came home to me just how much the fans value these events.

It was being held in the Mermaid Theatre, London, and was an afternoon featuring celebrity composers of the scores for detective thrillers. The drummer from 'The Shadows', Brian Bennett, who wrote the music for the Ruth Rendell series of TV dramas, was at the event. I was very much on the sidelines operating a tape machine[36] to play back examples of his work, and so never expected to be involved in any of the after show chat. I was packing up the gear, and walked through the foyer where members of the audience were chatting to the participants, including Brian Bennett. Two **Doctor Who** fans stopped me and asked for my autograph. They were thrilled to be getting a bonus signature at an event dedicated to something quite different, but they must have sensed my unease. I eventually had to own up.

"*You might find this odd,*" I said. "*But my musical education was kick started by playing Shadows instrumentals on a guitar, and I'll never forgive myself if I don't have a word with Brian Bennett, to tell him how much I owe him and The Shadows. Without them, I might never have had a musical career.*"

They certainly saw the funny side and graciously allowed me to leave them and cross the room to Brian Bennett where I'd behave just as they had done with me.

---

[36] Yes, it was a while ago!

BBC1 Christmas Jingles	October 1982	TV Presentation	BBC1
The Thirty-First of June	October 1982	Drama	Radio 4
Seeds of the Future	October 1982	Continuing Education	Radio 4
Computer Club	October 1982	TV Schools	BBC1
The Political Programme	November 1982	Current Affairs	BBC1
God in the Water	November 1982	Drama	Radio 4
The Human Brain	November 1982	BBC Enterprises	BBC
Animal Magic	December 1982	Network TV - Natural History Unit	BBC1
World Service Christmas	December 1982	World Service	External
Doctor Who (Serial 6K Special): The Five Doctors (Music)	April 1983	Drama Series and Serials TV	BBC1

The Five Doctors stands out because of its position in the cycle of my **Doctor Who** adventures. I'd already composed music for *The Leisure Hive*, *Warriors' Gate*, *Kinda*, and *Snakedance*, and had co-written a score for *Meglos* and *The King's Demons*. All that time, I'd been grappling with one big challenge: how to deliver music quickly and still produce sonically interesting material.

The Leisure Hive, being the first, gave me more time to work, and enjoyed some classical references, but the rest had been an exercise in inventing a focused soundworld that could be achieved with a minimum amount of technical resetting. In an age of little or no preset memories, changing things could be very labour intensive.

It was only when I came to *The Five Doctors* that I felt I'd mastered the technique. For this adventure, my studio contained the CS80, the early computer musical instrument The Fairlight, a Roland Voltage Controlled Sequencer playing the Roland 100M, and importantly a Roland sampler. I could call on a lot more firepower.

I made the rhythmic sound in the 'March of the Cybermen' by recording a series of different metallic sounds from objects like tape reels and waste paper bins, making them into samples, and performing them onto the multitrack. I then added another two performances on other tracks and mixed the three onto a stereo tape. This could then form the basis of all the Cybermen cues, and other synthesiser lines added to taste.

There were two breakthroughs for me: when I used samples of the original theme embedded in the music, and when I chose to make each strand of the story have a different sound. The scenes with Borusa, played by Philip Latham, would underpin the whole thing with Fairlight generated sounds based on time. A metronome-like sound constructed in the Fairlight is programmed on the composer page and then laid on to the multitrack. But what gives all these ideas perspective and provides the backdrop for all the action is that distant tower and the Horn of Rassilon.

I've mentioned many times in interviews how it was made. Rather than construct the whole thing from scratch, I sourced the basic sound from a BBC FX disc[37].

---

[37] They still feature this disc in the online archive of BBC Sounds at http://bbcsfx.acropolis.org.uk/?page=8&q=siren

There are several entries under the title 'R.M.S. Queen Elizabeth, ship's siren.' I used the first two. The first is straight, and the second has more rasp. They are two sounds clearly audible in the horn blasts, changing according to the velocity the key's struck on the sampler. The original sound has been raised in pitch with some harmonic distortion affecting the upper reaches, giving it more edge.

This is a great example of the three golden rules of successful sound design. You can summarise them as

- Source
- Performance
- Context.

I've already covered the first two, but the third is almost the most important. These scenes on the plain, with the Time Winds blowing and the tower in the distance, are reminiscent of many previous works.

The most well known is the Robert Browning poem, 'Childe Roland to the Dark Tower Came' and if you look on the Wikipedia page relating to that poem[38], there's a Victorian painting by the artist Thomas Moran[39] featured alongside which conjures up a very similar scene. It reminds us of previous mythical stories, and we are on the lookout for anything that confirms our worst suspicions. And along comes 'The Horn of Rassilon'.

It was a gift of a cue, one that only appears once in a while.

The Five Doctors was the only opportunity I had to write music for the Daleks or the Cybermen. It just so happened that all the other adventures I scored featured neither of the iconic adversaries. I also used the Fairlight in the Dalek scenes, only this time making a series of developing sounds constructed from unique sources. They were all very percussive in nature

---

[38] https://en.wikipedia.org/wiki/Childe_Roland_to_the_Dark_Tower_Came
[39] Currently, the painting is part of the collection of the Birmingham Museum of Art.

but with a rasping electronic edge.

I was pleased that the adventure went down so well with the viewers. It has gone through a few re-incarnations, including the splendid double album re-release by Silva Screen Records. If ever there was proof that artwork on a 12 inch sleeve makes it a collector's item, this is it. It's one of those projects I'm proud to have been involved with.

The Awakening

Radiovision The Astronomers	April 1983	Features, Art & Education	Radio 4 Schools	Incidental Music
Music Box	May 1983	DUP02 Radio Schools	Radio 4 Schools	
Seven Deadly Sins	July 1983	World Service	External Services	Signature Tune
Prima	August 1983	TV Continuing Education	BBC1	Incidental Music
Doctor Who (Serial 6M): The Awakening	September 1983	Drama Series and Serials TV	BBC1	Incidental Music

I remember seeing the very first Dalek episode when I was 14 years old, and was so enthralled by it that I couldn't wait until the next adventure to see more Daleks. Of course, that one was a two-part adventure entirely in the TARDIS, and the following one about Marco Polo was set in Central Asia in 1289 and ran for seven episodes. A very long time to wait for another Dalek.

So I've always regarded historical adventures as second best, but inevitably one arrived in my 'in' tray. *The Awakening* took place in the English Civil War and I approached it with trepidation, but help was at hand.

I've never been to an enjoyable BBC party. Shortly after starting to work on **Doctor Who**, the newspapers were running a story about the BBC allegedly spending too much licence payers' money on hospitality. So, in an attempt to shut the stable door, bolt it, bar it and fit a state-of-the-art security lock, the BBC made sure that its parties from then on were dismally unenjoyable.

The **Doctor Who** party in Madame Tussauds sounded exciting, until we entered the long rectangular function room. It could have been anywhere. The sandwiches tasted like props and stuck to the roof of your mouth. None of the promised celebs turned up, so we stood around with people we saw regularly at work and tried not to lapse into conversations about mixing and deadlines.

I should have been back in the studio starting work on *The Awakening*.

It was at that point I noticed the emergency exit at the back of the room. I persuaded two others that this was indeed an emergency and that we really needed to exit, and so we opened the door. Nobody saw us go.

As the door slammed behind us, we realised our mistake. It was very dark, with just one or two dim working lights around a large low-ceilinged area. The vague silhouettes of figures stood motionless in the space, and to our right, literally a few feet away, loomed Oliver Cromwell, flanked by two soldiers. We'd stepped right into the middle of the English Civil War. This Tussauds exhibition was closed for the night, and was spine tinglingly eerie. I now had a good idea what the characters in *The Awakening* were feeling. Perhaps the adventure wasn't so bad after all.

Planet of Fire

This should have been good. The location filming in Lanzarote provided some very effective backdrops, but somehow they just served as a constant reminder of how makeshift all the studio scenes were. To top it all, Peter Wyngarde was being asked to play a character with more than a passing resemblance to Lawrence of Arabia, but without the tension or the live camels!

As I've so often mentioned, I always try to find a unique feel for each adventure, and for this, dry and dusty was in order. I remember working with some shells picked up from Brighton beach many years before, and making Fairlight samples of their jangling. On this occasion, though, my modus operandi let me down. Producing dessicated music for a dessicated planet was far too literal. Something more figurative would have been better.

Thinking back to *Meglos* and the prickly cactus sound for the Doctor's violent rash, its success was, perversely, down to it not being the sound of a cactus! It was a sound that had associations with the *feel* of a cactus. With *Planet of Fire*, we were already in a rather one-dimensional world where almost everything related to fire. The music could have provided a welcome glimpse into something further, but unfortunately just delivered the same.

There's plenty of evidence that I was using more sophisticated resources, though. The Fairlight was used throughout, with some newer wavetable based synths. They supplied cutting runs and arpeggios, but these sounds were very short and sometimes too percussive. The director had wanted snappy short cues, and on occasions decided not to use music at all. Some scenes, such as Peri being rescued by Turlough, remained unscored, so that when music did arrive the brief punctuations took us by surprise instead of advancing the action.

Add to that the small TV loudspeakers found on most sets at the time, and you end up with a slight and ineffective score[40]. I remember, several years afterwards, compiling a single longer piece made up of a lot of the incidental music, which turned out very well. So, the content was there somewhere, but in such tiny bursts across all the programmes, you never got the chance to hear it as a whole.

The Two Doctors

As if to show his successors how it was done properly, Robert Holmes turned in a great script for *The Two Doctors*. I know there are some who feel that this is too frivolous at times, and too gory at others, but I think with such contrasts the action has more effect, and the scoring can make a difference.

In addition, there was one glaring, but overlooked, feature to this music: a real live musician. We were close to the orchestral management office on the top corridor at Maida Vale, and there was never any shortage of players. Since I joined the Workshop, I'd used session musicians to act as a foil for the electronic content. There was a cost involved, because working for us meant they would be doing 'outside work', not associated with their orchestral duties. Nevertheless, directors often felt that a live element in title or incidental music would add to its effectiveness.

Dudley Simpson had always used session players, because there was no realistic alternative, given the short deadlines. He would enhance the session music with the Synthi 100 at the Workshop, but the bulk of the sound was from live instruments. Not so in our era of **Doctor Who**. When we took over the incidental music, we regarded it as our brief to use electronic sources, and the directors expected it. But when *The Two Doctors* came along, there was not only a massive amount of location filming in Spain, but a lot of humour mixed into the action.

---

[40] I realise I am being hyper critical, but it's instructive to see the difference between what you thought at the time of composing, and what it sounds like now.

Patrick Troughton, on his last outing as the Doctor, and the wonderful John Stratton as Shockeye, deliver such engaging performances it would have been doing the adventure a great disservice to have scored it simply with electronics.

The director agreed. It was easy to imagine a classical guitar working in such a story, and I set about finding the player. A classical guitarist's not part of a symphony orchestra, so some research was necessary. Scoring for the Spanish guitar and running the session was challenging and very enjoyable. I was a folk and rock guitarist myself, but had never used a classical player. After all the other adventures I'd scored, I was keen to deliver something fresh and more emotional than before. The Workshop's music for **Doctor Who** had always been in a genre of its own. None of us saw it as part of the canon of work we were providing for other programmes, but something that demanded the 'house style' that Paddy Kingsland and I had set up six years before.

So, I look back on this one with some satisfaction, because it was able to break that mould. Whatever its reception by different groups of fans, I feel that all the elements of the adventure, script, acting, location, sound FX and music were in step, and we delivered a coherent piece of work.

The Two Doctors was my last **Doctor Who** adventure for television. Dudley Simpson had composed the music for the great majority of **Doctor Who** stories from 1964 to early 1980, and after John Nathan-Turner's arrival as Executive Producer, the newly equipped Radiophonic Workshop had taken over entirely[41]. Paddy Kingsland, Malcolm Clarke, Roger Limb and I had taken it in turns to cover every adventure from August 1980 to March 1985 with Elizabeth Parker[42] scoring one more two-part story later that same month. Thereafter, the reins were handed over to outside composers.

---

[41] A full list of **Doctor Who** composers can be found on Wikipedia.
[42] That story was *Timelash*, though she also provided special sounds for the Tom Baker adventure, *The Stones of Blood*. Elizabeth was more involved with that other scifi favourite, **Blake's Seven**.

We had a good stab at delivering a new musical sound to the programmes. I remember discussing with John Nathan-Turner the need to give the show a contemporary feel. Looking back now, what was contemporary then seems a bit 1980s and synth mad now, but that's what was called for at the time. Our newer technology had allowed us to have a stab at delivering sync'd music in a short space of time. For a rather slow worker such as myself, those adventures that had longer deadlines (*The Five Doctors*, for instance) resulted in more varied and inventive scores. In some ways, those original demos that Paddy and I had produced had 'set out a stall' which I found all too easy to rely on during those short turn rounds and late nights. When your music's due at the final mix in Television Centre the next morning, pressure can dim your creativity. I suppose I'd been spoilt during the six weeks I'd taken to deliver a remade title piece, but even now the more relaxed stories, such as *The Leisure Hive*, *Warrior's Gate*, and the *Five* and *Two Doctors* still have some pleasing cues for me.

It was going to be a full ten years before I had the chance to write more music for **Doctor Who**.

At last, HiFi Stereo

Throughout our time at the Workshop, there was one thing that made our hearts sink about working for TV. The pathetic speakers in television sets. I remember Dick Mills indulging in some plain speaking when he listened to one of my early **Doctor Who** cues.

"They'll never hear that bass, it'll just be a buzz."

The bass sounds in electronic music often lack the harmonics that a real instrument might have. These unadorned fundamentals were almost inaudible in TV speakers until the nineties[43].

---

[43] True, there were people who had invested in cinema style home sound systems, but we had to consider the average viewer.

"Never use the bottom notes of a bass guitar," Paddy had said to me. "It's a waste of time."

So, television restricted our sound palette.

Imagine my enthusiasm then, when I was approached to score two **Doctor Who** stories for radio. There was now a chance that they would hear the music properly.

The first, *The Paradise of Death* was broadcast in five episodes on BBC Radio 5. To my horror, I realised that, at that time, Radio 5 was only heard on AM. Hardly full frequency and still in Mono! Thankfully, they were repeated in April 1994 on Radio 2 FM, so all of my work was audible at last.

The second radio drama, *The Ghosts of N-Space*, was recorded in 1994 and finally broadcast in six parts on BBC Radio 2 in 1996.

Each of these adventures saw the very welcome return of Jon Pertwee to the role. Both of them also featured Elisabeth Sladen and Nicholas Courtney as Sarah Jane and the Brigadier.

At that time, there were two drama studios in BBC Maida Vale, MV6 and MV7. We'd all been very impressed by MV7's floor when it was installed. Because it was situated at the north-east corner of the long building, the designers were worried that the noise of the Bakerloo line, which ran underneath, might interfere with recordings. With that in mind, the entire floor of the studio was perched on massive coiled springs, a sort of giant mattress. As you walked across the floor of the studio, you could feel the bounce.

They were finishing the recording of *The Ghosts of N-Space* while I was upstairs putting the final touches to a different project. The studio downstairs ended their session before me, and most of them had dispersed, but by the time I'd shut down my gear and marched back down the long corridor to reception, there was one figure still left outside the front doors. Jon Pertwee had ordered a cab which had yet to turn up, and in the meantime a rain storm had descended on Delaware Road, leaving him stranded.

My car was parked a couple of blocks away, and so I too took refuge in the porch. Jon was as gracious as ever, but tired after a day's recording. The conversation was unremarkable, but I remember him complaining bitterly about his bad leg! When the rain eased, I said goodbye and left him waiting for the taxi.

It had not been the right moment to talk about **The Navy Lark**, **Worzel Gummidge**, or **Doctor Who**, even though they had formed such an important part of my early listening and viewing. Being stranded in a porch during a rainstorm waiting for a taxi doesn't fit well with the celebrity image. It's easy to forget how much mundane hard work goes into the things that entertain us. Just as much a job as anything else.

The Ghosts of N-Space was well received, and they had intended to produce a follow up, but in May of the following year Jon Pertwee died of a heart attack in America, and the run of Barry Letts-penned **Doctor Who** adventures came to an end.

My music for **Doctor Who** sits very clearly in the timeline of my compositions for the Workshop. It was such a special experience. At no other point did I score scifi at that length, and for an audience so tuned in to an entire universe of characters and stories. I was part of a relay race which is still being run today, and I only held the baton for a short time.

Bluedot

Should We be Here?

It's Saturday 8th July, 2017. We are playing at the Bluedot Festival today, in the shadow of the Jodrell Bank telescope, near Macclesfield.

I love sculpture trails, Anthony Gormley's statues, man-made objects in a rural setting, anything like that. The Jodrell Bank telescope's no sculpture, I admit, but its presence in the middle of rolling fields is a sight to behold. Sadly, today it has failed to achieve the familiar 72 degree angle, but remains staring straight upwards. There's something wrong with the motor. No doubt the engineer has been called.

The telescope's now a thriving tourist attraction, but its buildings and facilities have been given over to the Bluedot Festival, and we move our gear to our allotted stage through corridors of star maps and photos of galaxies. There's something romantic and epic about astronomy, and it seems an appropriate setting for music that aspires to be both romantic and epic, and a lot else besides. The stage we are to play on is impressive, and there's enough room for the audience out front, all enclosed inside a giant marquee. The entrances are so well sealed, light doesn't penetrate.

Our videos are going to look great.

Playing at festivals is a lucky dip. You get some that, despite being a festival, are performed across an entire city at different venues. Sheffield Sensoria was one of those, where we had the run of the whole theatre. In others, perhaps the majority, the full festival's happening on one big site, and the music is constant on different stages throughout the day. With these, you're loading your gear whilst another band's already playing[1]. It's like that today.

It happens so often that you become a little dismissive of what's being played. You're trying to focus on the matter in hand, making sure that our complicated rig is set and working, before being wheeled through the back drapes into position downstage. But, on this occasion, the music on stage seems curiously appropriate to our mood and for once does have an effect on us. So, once we've done the basic setup, we find our way to the side of the stage to see what's going on.

The band is The Plastic Mermaids. They are having a good gig, and playing well. The crowd's enjoying the moment, and their enthusiasm encourages the band to play better still. There's a girl looking on from the wings, enjoying it as much as we are. We assume she must be part of their crew; there are a few others doing the same thing. So it comes as a real surprise when after a few numbers she's introduced and goes on stage. It turns out that however good they've been till now, they are about to get even better. She has a trained operatic voice. You would think it inappropriate, but she soars over the top of their playing and quite literally takes everything to a new level.

It's time for our set. I've written a piece especially for Bluedot, with its intergalactic associations. The name of this has been a subject of constant banter throughout the rehearsals. Sometime a name just happens (we've

---

[1] It's not always a band though. I remember setting up behind the black drapes as John Cooper Clarke performed out front. None of us could concentrate. Such a funny, very cool guy, who just seems to get more so.

developed a new impro piece based on a riff by Kieron Pepper, for instance; the name 'Hula' seemed ideal and it stuck). Not so with this. We've been through everything, even 'Space Junk', and some unrepeatable rhyming slang for Jodrell Bank, but the solution came from Stephen Hawking.

His involvement with this piece was pure 'wishful thinking' to start with. I'd found a quote from his blockbuster *A Brief History of Time*…

Why is the universe the way we see it?
The answer is simple
If it had been any different
We would not be here

The piece needed some contrast half way through and so I mocked up the professor's voice saying these words, to see if it worked. It was effective but we couldn't use such well-known words without permission.

Mark said that he knew someone who worked with Prof. Hawking, and volunteered to sort it. To our enormous surprise, we not only got permission, but Stephen Hawking recorded the words himself. This is great for PR. We can now say that the number features the actual sound of one of the most famous scientists on the planet. It wasn't long before the problem with the name solved itself. The last line of the quote "We would not be here" became the title of the piece.

This didn't solve the banter at rehearsals. It now became known as 'Anywhere but here', 'We shouldn't be here' and everything in between.

I'm announcing the piece in the middle of the set, but when it comes to the name, I go into freeze mode. What if I call it one of the nicknames, especially one of the unrepeatable ones? The audience are in on the joke now, but by this time Mark has shouted it. It's easy for him, he's looking at the score.

Mark Ayres, Roger Limb, and Paul Hartnoll of the band Orbital, have written a new piece in Paul's studio, and Paul makes a guest appearance in our set to play a live version of the number, 'eShock'. He's already at the festival, because Orbital are headlining on the main stage tonight. One of their very popular tracks is a version of the **Doctor Who** title music, and we've been invited to appear with them. So, after our set and the inevitable packing up, we stay around for a second appearance, and it's going to be a bizarre experience.

We have each decided in advance to play a portable synthesiser. Mine is the Korg MS20. Owned and loved by Mark Ayres, who has pre-programmed a pokey bass sound. Mark has always wanted to stand on stage at a Festival with his Roland SH-101 slung around his neck. Now's his chance. He and I are due to be on the left side of the stage, whilst the others are on the right and up with Orbital on their raised platform. Anyone who has been to an Orbital gig will realise that they wear glasses with torches on each side. They look like luminous bog-eyed aliens peering at the crowd through clouds of stage smoke. To make our presence felt, we're going to have some as well.

We climb the stairs to the back of the stage and pick up a pair of earplugs out of a container by the door. This is going to be loud. There's a roadie standing in front of a table covered with a black cloth, the component parts for the headsets laid out in rows in front of him. Black plastic glasses with no lenses, a lot of pencil torches, and two reels of Sellotape. The guy's really enjoying constructing these things; he's beaming from ear to ear. First the batteries go into the torches and are switched on, the torches get Sellotaped to the glasses, and the final headset gets laid in a row on the table. The roadie has seen us walk up and is pleased to have an audience. The problem is, he isn't able to take the leap from making the glasses to handing them out. His leaping powers might be hampered by what he's smoking. A colleague comes up and barks at him over the music.

"What are you doing? Give them the bloody glasses!"

The roadie hands them over; still not entirely sure what just happened.

Mark and I take up our positions. There's an enormous crowd out there, enjoying every minute, but it's hard for me to feel part of it. There's a lot of smoke, I feel dwarfed by the platform that Orbital are performing on, and my hearing's somewhat compromised by the two yellow polystyrene bungs that are wedged in my ears. I feel as if I'm on board a ship in a storm. Either way, I don't feel ready to play the bass part of **Doctor Who** on an MS20. Phil Hartnoll shouts down, asking if we are all set. I give him a thumbs up. I am lying.

The number starts. We play. There's a foldback speaker in front of me, I assume that the sound of my synthesiser is coming out of it. It's a bit late to find out. The crowd are going wild and enjoying every minute. I'm wondering if I'm switched on. I find the volume knob on the synthesisers and turn it up. Yes, I'm definitely switched on; that was really loud. The music carries us to the end of the track in a dreamlike state. The crowd erupts. We turn in their direction, wave, and head off the stage.

I'm convinced it was a total disaster, but the feedback from front of house is very positive. It's only the next day when I see the amazing amount of publicity it has generated and the striking videos on YouTube that I realise what that was all about. One of them captures that split second when I give Orbital the thumbs up; I look like one of the stokers in the engine room giving the all clear. The stage is populated with shadowy figures whose eyes beam out through the smoke; they are tinkering around on strange devices like cartoon workers down a mine. It's an other-worldly sight, but this was special in another way. Here were Orbital, the latest purveyors of Ron Grainer's iconic music, jamming with the Radiophonic Workshop, the original ones, live in front of a sellout audience beside the Jodrell Bank telescope in the dark of a summer night.

Down Time

Back in the days of regular salaried employment, our eyes were constantly on the clock. Almost all TV work came with the stress of deadlines. Having to rewrite unsatisfactory material, the most unwelcome of outcomes, led to impossibly long days. So, any chance to unwind was welcome, and breaking for coffee, lunch and the inevitable tea was more than sustenance. It kept us going.

The restaurant behind reception became an important part of our working lives.

The canteen had previously had a terrible reputation. In its early days, it was something to be avoided, but by the time I arrived at the BBC, things had looked up on the culinary front. Still not Masterchef, but not Little Chef either. There were more places to eat in Broadcasting House, and the restaurant on the eighth floor, with its view across All Souls Church towards Oxford Street offered a welcome break from the windowless world that we all inhabited whilst working in the studios.

When I left Broadcasting House to work for three months at the BBC building in Maida Vale, I was disappointed to find a canteen with no windows or atmosphere. Just a few solitary people sipping tea.

I was wrong to be disappointed.

The very long building contained a wide variety of studios. On any one day you might see actors, classical singers, crooners, orchestral musicians, rock musicians, big band musicians, jazz players and of course members of the Radiophonic Workshop. They all had one thing in common; the need to escape the claustrophobia of their studios. In addition, there were the creative, technical and office staff from orchestral management, studio management, engineering department, and the film department (yes, there was a film department in radio).

Everybody was there for the same reason, to have a few minutes talking about something else. Anything other than the play, the Radio 2 show, the John Peel Session, the symphony, the piano recital or the latest radiophonic conundrum that had preoccupied them all the morning.

All of them, bar us, worked in groups. Even the solo piano recital used an engineer in the control room, and a producer alongside, but we will have worked on our own. There was almost no collaboration with other members of our department. Although I do remember a couple of occasions when Roger Limb kindly played some jazz for me. He's an accomplished jazz player and it would have been ridiculous to supply it myself[2]. Also, there were occasions when my work with a score needed some outside assistance. The main theme of the film *Life Story* was based on music by another composer[3], and Roger helped decipher some of the parts for me. Those occasions stand out because they were so infrequent, and we spent most of the time working on our own.

A rather monastic existence, but then no different from a graphic artist, a painter or any creative person. It's a matter of practicality, really. Nobody wants to sit at the back of a room while someone painstakingly adds one more brush stroke, one more wash, one more phrase to a slowly evolving work. None of us liked the idea of anyone doing that, either.

So, around one o'clock the corridors became busy again and everyone headed towards the canteen. Of all those disparate groups of diners, nothing compared to the massed hordes from Studio One, the home of the BBC Symphony Orchestra. We could look down on them from the top corridor, through the glass of the balcony doors. They worked to strict schedules, but the precise time that they broke for lunch was up to the conductor of the day, and the length of the piece they were rehearsing. Some knowledge of the classics was helpful. If you could recognise the

---

[2] I'm certainly OK with spontaneous playing, but it falls short of the clever harmonic moves you find in jazz.
[3] Such occasions were rare, and, as in the case of **Doctor Who**, the original composer would be credited at the end of the programme and in all the programme documentation.

closing bars of Beethoven's *Eroica Symphony*, or Grieg's *Piano Concerto*, you were in with a chance. As soon as the last note sounded, the musicians stampeded for the studio door and the rush to beat them was on. Too late, and you'd be behind up to eighty hungry musicians.

The canteen was a welcome release, and the scene of many flights of fancy, anecdotes, and gossip.

One Monday, completely without warning, a maggot sticking out of a large green apple greeted us from the side wall of the canteen. The management had clearly decided that something light-hearted looking down on us as we ate would cheer us up. Salads didn't sell well that day, and various complaints were lodged.

It was clear that the decision had been hasty and ill thought through, so by the Wednesday a smiley face had been added to the maggot, to show that he bore us no ill will, and that should we come across him in any of the fruit, and accidentally bite his head off, we would know that he had been happy right up to the end.

Further complaints were lodged. Two days later a red hat had been added to the maggot's smiley face, which gave the impression that this was no accidental intrusion, and he was intent on making a day of it.

Even more complaints arrived, mostly from people who had had their sense of humour removed.

The following Monday, the whole wall had been re-emulsioned, and the happy maggot had gone. Although it's cheering to know that even to this day he waits in hiding, ready to mystify another generation of diners. The management vowed never to venture into the unpredictable world of fine art again, but their plans were thwarted when, some years later, the BBC was building their 'White City' site. This was up the road from Television Centre and had all the aesthetic appeal of a pile of shoeboxes. To get planning permission for this development, the council had allegedly insisted that it should feature a work of art somewhere in its design. The BBC commissioned a sculptor whose work is evident to this day. It consists of a series of rafters leaning against one another like the skeleton of a wigwam. Inside them, there hangs a dull metal globe with continents jutting out of it. From a passing car on the Westway alongside, it looks rather like a wrecking ball; no doubt available at a moment's notice if ever they fancy knocking the whole place down.

I think it was to celebrate the fortieth anniversary of BBC2.

Before many of the programmes that night, viewers would be treated to a specially designed animated logo with accompanying music. I drew the short straw on this one and had to come up with something. Elsewhere in this book, I go on about how I need some dramatic context as a starting point for a piece of music. To the management of BBC2 it might have seemed like a dramatic event, but to me it was about as dramatic as… well, something that wasn't dramatic at all[4]. Judging by the standard of the visuals, the graphic designer agreed with me.

Once completed, my music for this logo had fallen at every possible hurdle; sound, music, recording, mixing, appeal of any sort. It purely served as a placeholder to tell the viewers that their TV speakers were functioning, nothing more.

It was always a disappointment in the canteen that whenever any of your music had been on TV the night before, music that you were particularly proud of, not one person in the whole place had even watched the programme, let alone liked the music.

Which is why I was rather taken aback when Richard Attree took

---
[4] Trying to write music for Michael Palin as he went through the turnstile on the Tokyo underground, only to find his ticket wouldn't work, came a close second. Not exactly *Star Wars*.

the trouble to tell everyone that last night he had heard just about the worst piece of music he had ever experienced, accompanying the 40th Anniversary logo on BBC2.

Luckily, and to prove my point, no one else had even watched BBC2 the night before, and I carved away at my pork chop, hoping the whole thing would blow over. Because Richard was the only person to have heard this travesty, that's exactly what happened, and the subject turned to just about anything as long as it wasn't music.

To this day Dick Mills and I try to tell this joke in public. It has never been very successful. I remember us trying it out in Barking. One of the celebrity actors[5] had encouraged us, but the joke didn't travel well; it certainly didn't like going to Barking.

It was created way back in the BBC Canteen at Maida Vale, around a table in the far corner. Present were Malcolm Clarke, Dick Mills and myself. All three of us idly looking for something to delay our return to the studios.

Conversation lurched from one subject to another. By some circuitous route, we ended up talking about circuses. All three of us agreed that circuses were fundamentally boring. Seen one, seen them all. What they really needed was an injection of original acts. Clowns with a car that worked, that sort of thing.

The conversation turned to animal acts.

I suggested that using unusual animals would be a start.

We each suggested an animal. I think I suggested a hippopotamus. Malcolm came up with a giraffe, and Dick, a pelican.

---

[5] His card has been marked.

We sat there picturing this unholy trio; a giraffe, a hippopotamus and a pelican. After a good while, Malcolm asked.

"What does the pelican do?"

"Oh," said Dick without hesitation. *"He holds the giraffe's trousers."*

Well, I told you it didn't travel. Perhaps what makes it slightly original is that unlike jokes that have a three-stage story, this one leaps from stage one to the payoff, leaving us to fill in the gaps. We have to visualise the unlikely copulation, whilst the pelican, who must have felt like a gooseberry right from the start, ends up having to hold the giraffe's trousers.

We keep on trying to retell this joke, convinced that its failure has been down to poor storytelling, but the truth is that to get its full value, you should have been there.

The canteen remains almost unchanged. I hope they've replaced the carpet, but I'm not sure. That wall is still whitewashed, with the maggot lurking beneath. It still looks painfully dull and underlit, but just as before, comes alive once the customers appear. Sadly, there's no longer a working drama studio at Maida Vale, and so the actors and directors have gone, and with them all the outrageous chatter. However, the variety of musicians remains, the rock stars mingling with the opera singers and gentlemen of the orchestra. But somehow, it's lost its spark. With all those precious artists in one room, all released from their studios, there'd been a sense of fun. Sure, we all had our eye on the clock, but for that concentrated hour, we were celebrating.

Don't Roll Your Rs

The BBC building at Maida Vale defined our working world. It was easy to imagine that anything you dreamed up within those walls could come to pass. This rather childlike approach to creativity had its casualties, but now and then an idea would show some promise. I'd found an excellent translation of the Italian classic, Dante's *Inferno*. It featured the original Italian on the left page, and the English on the right. Even to someone with the most basic knowledge of Italian, it was clear that the sound of the poetry was amazing, and the narrative vividly theatrical; ideal for an audio-only production. I decided to set it in modern times. The listener is one of a group of tourists being shown round the burnt-out pit by a modern day guide. Of course, as we descend into this ruin, we realise that the old Hell is still there, and our guide is Satan himself.

Around that time, I was having to make regular trips to Sheffield, and on each occasion spent some time in Sheffield Library doing some research. It was a very quiet and effective place to work, containing plenty of material on Dante and **The Divine Comedy**[6]. One book, *Dante–the Maker* by William Anderson, seemed particularly useful. It was an in-depth look at the creative process which lead to *Inferno*. It brought Dante's actual act of writing into the present, and helped me realise that a modern version would be possible. I knew that a script had to be written based on the original, so I wondered if I could meet the author to discuss a collaboration.

To my surprise, William Anderson agreed to meet[7] the very next week. From the start, I knew we could work well together. We both had a real interest in creativity, and he thought my ideas were worth pursuing. It was going so smoothly, but then he said, "*There's a bit of a problem. My head is just not in the right place to be involved with the* Inferno *at the moment. I've fallen in love. For me,* Paradiso *would be more appropriate.*"

How could I disagree?

---

[6] **The Divine Comedy** is a three part series of works by Dante depicting his journey through Hell (Inferno), up through Purgatory (Purgatorio), into Heaven (Paradiso).

[7] The BBC's name must have had an enormous influence on his accepting the invitation. I must have been completely unknown to him.

It was a lovely meeting, and must have given me some encouragement, because shortly afterwards I decided to write the adaptation myself.

Inferno Revisited would be what the Performing Rights Society call a musico-dramatic work. A piece where neither the music nor the speech has precedence, but where the narrative is advanced by both.

The parallel texts in Italian and English were proving very inspiring. I featured as many spoken or sung excerpts from the Italian as possible, and chose which scenes from the original I'd use as inspiration for the adaptation. It looked as if it would last around 45 minutes. Things were progressing OK, but I was to receive an unexpected shock.

The idea had been accepted in principle by Radio 4, but there was no planned broadcast date. Suddenly, without warning, Radio 4 informed us that there was a suitable slot, but it was only six weeks away.

I took the plunge and agreed. A lot of the scenes were already in sketch form, so the deadline seemed achievable.

Firstly, a tightly scheduled 'to do' list would be necessary.

I would need to record a working performance of the Satan/guide character using a BBC Repertory actor to serve as a reference during the assembly of the programme. Music and sound in such a strong narrative would always need to respond to the words, and with a rough performance in place, I could shape the sounds and music around the rhythm of the speech.

A second session would be needed with the group of tourists (all played by members of BBC Radio Repertory), and a further one with Singcircle, who had agreed to supply all the choral content.

A large session with a string orchestra would have to be slotted in somewhere. This was to cover one particular section of the narrative.

A final session would then be necessary with the actor who'd play the guide and Satan in the finished piece. A mix could then take place in MV4, to put the whole thing together ready for broadcast.

So with a tight plan in place, I could get down to the work. But there was one other complication.

I was trying to move flats at the time, and due to various negotiations falling through, I found myself with nowhere to live for three or four months. I needed a short lease on a flat within a reasonable distance of Maida Vale, so that I could easily continue my work on *Inferno*. After a few disastrous viewings, I came across a basement close to Primrose Hill, just off Regent's Park Road. It was a short drive from work and was a really unusual set of rooms. I learnt that the owner, who would be abroad for three months, was half Russian and half Italian. In keeping with her ancestry, the lady turned out to be a mixture of extrovert and darkly moody and was excited by the thought of so much Dante being read and recited in her absence.

Her presence remained in the flat long after she had left. Italian influenced pictures looked down from the walls, and ornaments from further east shone out from ornate glass cabinets. I worked at a large dining table covered in a dark velvet cloth.

On my first morning, I woke to an unusual sound. The window was open, and the residents of Regents Park Zoo could be heard in the distance; the wonderful exotic cries from a vast collection of animals waking from sleep. But there was another cry, this one far less pleasant. Definitely human, but a human in some distress, and it was getting closer. A moaning that seemed to go on and on. After a while, other sounds joined in, clattering and scraping. It was the binmen. One of whom, clearly in his own special world, enjoyed 'singing'. Every Monday morning the same thing would happen. To him it was a wonderful sound, but I was deep in the Inferno, and to me it was a cry of pain.

A very intense six weeks followed. The studio still had a rather disparate collection of unconnected gear, but it did include the Fairlight and many odd boxes, so I was convinced I could pull this off.

Brian Hodgson had kindly agreed to produce the programme for me, which meant I could concentrate more on the writing. First of all, we recorded the reference performance of the guide's voice. Next, a session in Studio MV4 was arranged to record all the crowd content. These days, in feature films, actors often complain about spending their whole day in front of a green screen[8], without any idea how their performance will fit into the final production. This suffered from the same problem. The poor actors were performing to instructions without any context. My instructions became more and more insistent. One poor actress, instructed to scream at the opening of one scene, begged me to stop asking for retakes as she had no more scream left in her.

The sessions with Singcircle came next[9]. They were well known in contemporary music circles for their stunning live delivery, and to achieve it, relied heavily on their conductor, Gregory Rose. Expecting them to listen to a metronome click in headphones (the normal studio technique), would result in rather stilted performances, and so some interface between the audio tracks and their conductor was essential. So, I enlisted the help of the engineers to create what would eventually be called the 'Electric Baton'.

These days such an idea would be two hours' work on a laptop and the use of an iPad in front of the conductor. Then, without the universal language of a computer, the device had to be put together with hardware

---

[8] Any performances in front of a green screen allow the background and many other things to be added later.
[9] Singcircle, one of the leading vocal groups in Europe, performed their last concert—a rendition of *Stimmung* by Stockhuasen—in 2017, at the Barbican.

components from scratch. It ended up as three illuminated slits in a metal box. The three lights were driven by pitches recorded on the multitrack tape. The rhythm of the pitches simulated the movement of a baton. So for 4/4 meter, you'd see the vertical light for the downbeat, bottom left for the second beat, bottom right for the third, and the bottom right and the upright for the fourth or upbeat. The problem with this was its size—the idea was fine, but its execution was Lilliputian.

Both singers and conductor were very patient with this rather odd device, a lot more so than Malcolm Clarke, who took the trouble to tell everyone at one of our monthly meetings how utterly ridiculous it was. I was happy to put up with the ridicule, however, because it did result in good performances.

Almost all of their libretto was Italian, and a previous Workshop composer, Maddalena Fagandini volunteered to help. She was a native Italian speaker, and only too eager to put the singers right on some important points, especially when to roll their r's. They were rolling them all the time. It's one of those over regimented habits of a strict vocal training that I also found irritating. Maddelena was at pains to point out that the Italians only roll on double r's not on every single one.

"Rolling your r's on every occasion just sounds ridiculous," she told them.

They started another take, and she would be opening the door to the studio before they had finished.

"Stop rolling the bloody r's. Why are you doing it? It's stupid!"

They were going to have to break the habit of a lifetime, otherwise this passionate Italian was not going to let them go home. They obliged, and peace broke out.

I'm glad to say that Singcircle didn't over-indulge in vibrato either. Heard often in instrumental playing, it's especially prevalent in singing. The rhythmic wobbling around a pitch is supposed to enhance the sound but for me, it makes it impossible to listen to. Singcircle was celebrated for its performances of Stockhausen, and in that kind of music pitches have to be pitches, not some vague approximation[10].

The material from Singcircle still stands out today as being amongst the best content of the whole piece.

There was a breakout section in the middle of *Inferno Revisited* which mirrored one in the original. There are many examples of using contrast in creative work. Attention can be drawn to the quality of the main theme by taking us somewhere else that's a complete change. I've already mentioned the Middle 8 of Ron Grainer's **Doctor Who** theme as being refreshing in that way. This is not a new idea. Shakespeare would use a scene with a comic character in the middle of a tragedy, but Dante pulls off one of the most audacious breakouts ever.

We have spent all this time going ever deeper into the circles of Hell, but progress is barred at the gates until the appearance of an angel from Heaven. This white winged creature glides above the surface of the marsh, and brings everyone to their knees. The presence of something divine in Hell, is such a wonderful idea. We're so transfixed by the image that when the angel leaves, the dismal and tragic nature of Hell seems even more poignant.

Clearly, the scene needed something surprising and different. I decided to use a string orchestra. Every other musical ingredient in the piece had been made or manipulated through electronics, and suddenly we would be confronted with a sound that was real and live, with no tricksy effects. It was a hard thing to accomplish in those six short weeks, but with some help from an arranger and the conductor, I managed to write and

---

[10] Whilst at the National Film and Television School, I had the chance to record a Viol da Gamba. Played without vibrato, it is the purest instrumental sound I have ever heard.

produce the piece in time. I'd written the piece in a very English, Vaughan Williams-like style and the orchestra captured it perfectly.

So all was now assembled, as we entered the last two weeks of the project.

When I started at the BBC, I was a studio manager working in small radio productions for the schools department, but the roll call of actors taking part was impressive. Derek Jacobi, Bernard Hepton, Judi Dench and many others were often seen in the Portland Place studios. There were no lines to learn; it was radio. There was little pressure, either. The producer, so grateful to have such luminaries in his production, just let them get on with it. They were on their way to the West End for their evening performances and were only too happy to oblige.

We had sent Alec McCowen the script, in the hope that he too would value stopping off on his way to work, and he got back to us in a few days to accept.

He was a lovely man to work with. We were in the studio, morning and afternoon, carefully working through the script, scene by scene. He had already prepared some ideas ahead of the recording, so we completed everything in two or three takes. We broke for lunch around 12.30, and just after one o'clock whilst sitting around a table in the canteen, he said he was returning to the studio to have a sleep on the floor for half an hour. This was a regular habit whenever he was appearing in the West End in the evening. It was a habit of mine, too. I'd often take a power nap on the studio floor in order to work through the night, so I quite understood.

I threaded Alec McCowen's performance into the sounds and music and set about preparing all the tracks for the final mix.

The programme was to be broadcast on April 17th, 1983. On April 9th, the printing works which handled the *Radio Times* had a dispute with the BBC, and failed to print the next edition, the one that listed[11] *Inferno*. It was very unwelcome news, and something which must have depressed the listening figures, although it's impossible to say by how much.

That disappointment at the time of broadcast was short-lived, because subsequently it became a bit of a cult thing. But I've been used to little-known events that slowly gather interest ever since the early seventies, when the five albums with John Ferdinando went from a tiny distribution to being collectors items. They've even been re-issued as a CD box set[12].

Inferno Revisited was re-issued by the BBC Transcription Service, and distributed amongst many overseas outlets. It still crops up online. To date, it's my only broadcast script, and something I'm pleased to have done.

There's enormous satisfaction in originating an idea and then seeing it all the way through to a completed work. The Radiophonic Workshop band wrote a half hour tribute to the moon landings in 2019, which gave us the same sense of achievement.

---

[11] The listing that would have been printed can be found on the BBC Genome website. http://genome.ch.bbc.co.uk/931a2c20d56a4b2fbb41a186e9b8675b

[12] From Cherry Red Records. https://www.cherryred.co.uk/product/a-game-for-all-who-know-the-hf-recordings-box/

The National Portrait Gallery

Just Take The Lift

It's the 20th January, 2017. We are playing at the National Portrait Gallery today.

Not a venue you'd expect for performances of electronic music, but there's a good reason. They are running an exhibition to do with Picasso, and have invited various artists of every persuasion to perform late on a Friday evening all around the gallery. They've allocated us the lecture theatre, because of the complex setup. It has a small stage and seating for one or two hundred people. We set about rigging the gear and tuning our sound to the room.

Normally the exit to the dressing area is upper stage left, but a large video projection screen on the rear wall has obscured it.

"*Don't worry,*" says the stage manager, "*you can use the door on the other side. There's a lift immediately to your right which will take you down to the dressing room level.*"

That all sounds simple enough, and we get back to our rig and check out the circuits.

We are due to play a twenty-minute piece twice during the evening with an hour's gap in between each performance. The first one goes smoothly. Somewhat of a relief, because this is the first time we've co-written a piece of that length in such a short time. Early preparation involved dividing the twenty-minute piece into sections and further into cues and arranging tempos and keys in advance. With all that pre-prepared, we've put together nineteen minutes of semi-improvised music in just three days' rehearsal. The piece goes down well and we exit through the designated door. The space is cramped, and it's hard for the whole band to leave the stage at once. To our right, stands the lift.

Ah, the lift! It's a disabled lift with glass doors and large buttons to operate. It only travels a distance of eight or nine feet down to the lower level. We have to take turns, as it only holds three people at a time. After a few trips, we all find ourselves in the dressing room in good spirits. Various guests have come backstage to find us and everyone's enjoying themselves. Our manager comes in after a while, to tell us that we need to be back on stage in a few minutes for our second performance, and after emptying our glasses we find our way back to the base of the lift. Kieron, our drummer, has already gone up, and is waiting for the rest of us on the upper level. Mark, Roger, and Paddy climb into the lift. They get the thing moving, but it stops halfway up. We are all good at buttons, in fact our stage act features rather a lot of them, but these very big ones on the side of the lift have defeated the three occupants. A discussion breaks out. Should they push and hold the big red one or just jab it? Kieron, who can see everything unfolding from the upper level, is recording it on his phone. The rest of us stand in the basement witnessing the drama unfold. In the meantime, two hundred people are waiting in the auditorium ready to welcome the Radiophonic Workshop, unaware that it's wedged in a disabled lift, just behind a door to the left of the stage. It isn't clear what gets the lift moving. Perhaps being Japanese and fully computerised, it needs to check with Head Office in Tokyo, but for whatever reason, it finally budges and we all make it up to stage level.

Our second performance isn't as good as the first. It's a fairly thoughtful piece, and not best served by wedging the performers in a lift before playing it[13].

Treading Water

Back in the day, though, our working lives were not so convivial. Much of our time would be spent in our own studios, sometimes long after everyone else had gone. I remember **Junior Electronics** being a very solitary experience, for instance.

Snowflake '83	October 1983	TV Presentation	BBC1	Jingles
Woofer (Ep1 to 5)	November 1983	TV Children	BBC1	Incidental Music
Horizon: Parasites	November 1983	TV Science Features	BBC2	Incidental Music
Junior Electronics	November 1983	Features, Arts & Education	Radio 4 Schools	Signature Tune

"It's a bit of a strange project, this," said the producer. It was Arthur Vialls from Schools Radio. "We're running a series of programmes about electronics, and I'd like you to provide the opening music."

Nothing strange, so far, but then he added, "...and you need to play it on this oscillator."

He'd walked in with a large holdall and dived into it enthusiastically,

---

[13] Still, the whole evening must have gone down well, because Warp Records released the piece a short time afterwards under the title *Everything You Can Imagine is Real*.

revealing a small printed circuit board, crammed with components.

"*You see, during this series of programmes, we ask each student to make an oscillator just like this,*" he said. "*I want to tell them you used the same thing in the title music.*"

His eyes moved from the pegboard of bits in his hand to the array of gear around the studio.

"*Bit of a David and Goliath situation, I know, but see what you can do. Use this BBC paper cup as a loudspeaker.*"

He switched the device on, and it emitted a pitched buzz.

"*If you approach it with your hand, the pitch will go up,*" he added, helpfully.

There was already an electronic instrument, the Theremin, which changed pitch in the same way. But the theremin sensed your approaching hands as they interfered with the earthing of the signal, whereas light triggered this device to sound. The more you obstructed the light over it, the lower the pitch[14].

It was basic to say the least, but Delia Derbyshire had created the ground breaking **Doctor Who** music just using oscillators for the top line, so what could possibly go wrong?

I decided to use this on the top line as well, and set about writing a fairly obvious poppy bass riff as an accompaniment. In fact, in the end, the oscillator wasn't used for the main theme, but as answering phrases. I discovered that by moving my hands in very fast waves around a central position I could simulate vibrato. More than that, when echo was added, it resembled a rather hysterical operatic soprano, scatting around the top

---

[14] With the Theremin it was the reverse. The closer, the higher the pitch.

of her range[15]. No-one pretended that this was a sophisticated musical instrument, so the tongue-in-cheek style would go down well.

The real problem came right at the end of the piece.

I needed a final low note as the ultimate full stop to the music, but however much I obscured the oscillator with my hand, my whole body, or even a cloth, it still wouldn't emit a low enough note. I turned off the studio lights. No joy. The multitrack machine had bright lights on the display, and so I switched it off. Still not low enough. Finally, I turned off the lights in the corridor outside, to stop light coming under the door.

Success.

Now the only complication was that I couldn't see where the Record button was because the studio was pitch black, and so had to put the lights back on, press the button, turn all the lights off, and record the note onto a separate piece of tape.

An escapade worthy of Mr Bean.

I'm glad to say that when the producer returned a week later, he was delighted, and away he went with the master tape in his holdall.

I moved on to the next project and never heard it broadcast. I never heard whether anyone else liked it. No one in the department heard it. In fact, I didn't hear it again until I was putting together tracks for a Silva Screen retrospective, and remembered all the antics.

There were so many moments like this; little one-off requests that were just taken for granted. After all, it was why we were there, but it's sad to think that so many will be forgotten.

---

[15] My dislike for vibrato doesn't apply here. This is fun, and a long way from classical music!

Some things were more memorable than others, however.

The Next President	September 1980	Current Affairs/ Special Projects	BBC TV
Turning Points	October 1980	TV Science Features	BBC2
You and Yours Victorian Signature Tunes	November 1980	Current Affairs and Magazine Progs	Radio 4
The Making of Mankind (Reel 1 of 3)	December 1980	TV Science Features	BBC2

It would wrong to suggest that we were entirely marooned in Delaware Road. Our involvement in television had broadened our horizons in more ways than one. Not only were we always required to attend final mixes at Television Centre, but when working on filmed documentaries[16], we often visited cutting rooms to deliver our latest music.

This cutting room was in a rather rundown residential house in Baron's Court, just off the Great West Road in London. These places always had the same feel, damp unloved spaces with peeling paintwork, and editing gear in almost every room. Film editing was a long-winded affair, and paying for better premises was never an option. These private cutting rooms were often run by ex-BBC employees who had set up within striking distance of the big house (Television Centre).

Graham Massey, the director, met me at the top of the stairs and showed me into what must have been a master bedroom once, but was now furnished with a six plate Steenbeck, Pic-Sync, and racks of film dangling on cup hooks. This was the post production home of **The Making of**

---

16 And there were many of these: **The Body in Question, Horizon, Everyman, Timewatch** and many more.

Mankind, a seven-part series tracing the origins of our species, presented by Richard Leakey.

"Have a seat," he said. "We'll be with you shortly, but we're just trying to sort out this problem with a reconstruction."

The viewing screen showed a scene shot on an African savanna, featuring native figures moving through long grass, holding spears.

"This was a nightmare to shoot," he said. "They wouldn't remove their underpants."

The editor and I clearly found this funnier than the director, who became quite animated.

"We told their agent they would have to be naked, but they just refused. I wouldn't mind, but they're red. The underwear. We tried to shoot through long grass but as you can see, there are still red blotches visible."

It would be another four or five years before any sort of computer graphics emerged, and many more years before red underpants could be painted out digitally. The series was being made in the twilight period of film, when the old techniques held sway and things were still a little rough and ready. I remember the director and I standing in front of a microphone in the foley booth, grunting and stamping our feet in sync with the picture, as the underpanted Neanderthals crept over the savanna.

For every one of these programmes, I held an instrumental recording session. Often, when programme budgets were small, we would record a session with one player, and provide the rest of the score in our studios. On this occasion, I used a flute player, but to make the sound more in keeping with the subject, scored it for concert and alto flute, a longer and deeper sounding instrument. Because every session was run according to Musicians' Union guidelines, the player received an augmented fee for playing two instruments. Besides the session fees, the agreement also entitled him to residuals or royalty payments each time the programme was broadcast. The series was repeated once during the initial period, but because of its popularity, once again six months later. I met the flautist in the Maida Vale canteen about a year afterwards. He saw me and came over.

"Thanks for the motor launch!" he said.

During this period, we often scored high profile series which broadcast to ever increasing audiences who became interested in the equipment we were using. Sensing a business opportunity, manufacturers of the latest electronic goodies were beating our door down, trying to get their products endorsed.

We'd assemble in the 'Piano Room'[17], to see the latest fads.

On one occasion, there was a guy extolling the virtues of the eBow. This hand held device extracts sustained notes and weird harmonics from an electric guitar[18]. The salesman greeted us with a typical piece of spiel.

"As of now," he said, "*the synthesiser is redundant.*"

After a while we tired of the frequent demonstrations, and so were expecting to dismiss the Fairlight CMI as well.

"*The amazing thing about this bit of gear,*" said the salesman with unstoppable delight, "*is that you'll never ever need to replace the hardware. All you need to do is keep the software up to date, via these floppy disks.*"

He brandished an eight inch flexible piece of plastic in a cardboard sleeve.

---

[17] The largest room in the Workshop and our acoustic recording area.
[18] Paddy Kingsland still uses one in our concerts.

The sleeve had two holes in it. One in the centre (sort of essential), and another slot shaped hole somewhere on the surface of the disk to allow the computer to read the data. He pushed it into the drive slot, and the Fairlight came to life.

It looked intriguing, but its computing power was slight by modern standards. It was capable of sampling a maximum of 6 seconds of sound across the whole machine, and then only in 8 bit[19]. This was not the brave new world, but to us it seemed like all our Christmases had come at once. For years we'd been cutting up pieces of tape and re-assembling them to make chickens sing and corks play tunes. Now with the Fairlight, such important and intellectually challenging tasks could be achieved in a fraction of the time. We were so excited with this recent acquisition that, on the day of its arrival, we set it up in the Workshop's smallest room, without windows or air, and played with it for a very long time. The secretary knocked on the door.

"Do you realise it's 6 o'clock? You haven't come out of here for hours. Not even for tea!"

When we failed to go for tea, people feared the worst. In fact, we'd just been making a dog bark in several octaves, and a stick of celery play 'God Save the Queen'. The licence fee was safe.

There had been a choice around that time between two high value items: the Fairlight Computer Music Instrument, and the Synclavier. The latter was a tempting and comprehensive mixed mode synthesiser, which these days still graces our screens as part of the **Casualty** theme music, written by Ken Freeman, but otherwise seems to have bitten the dust[20]. In the end, we plumped for the Fairlight because of its sampling facilities and also its in-built composer page.

---

[19] A very basic quality of digital recording, reserved these days for so called lo fi effects. Very prone to an ugly distortion, because it has to approximate so much of the audio.
[20] Although it does still appear in digital form as an instrument plug in.

Although the Fairlight was never the permanent solution that the salesman had predicted, it represented a turning point. I often used it as part of a bigger ensemble of sounds, such as in **Doctor Who**'s *Snakedance*, and *The Five Doctors* adventures. In our search today for perfect resolution and clean sound, it's easy to forget that sometimes it's the character in a sound that makes it memorable rather than its quality. Nobody could pretend that the Mellotron, with its keyboard driven tape loops, offered perfect reproduction, but its flute sound is unique and original. The iconic opening of The Beatles' 'Strawberry Fields Forever' would be lost without it.

There was no doubt about the Fairlight's importance to us. It was a watershed moment.

The day that many soothsayers had foretold when the VCS3 synth arrived sixteen years before had finally come to pass. The Fairlight had replaced the need to re-pitch and cut up tape. We would no longer need to use John Baker and Delia Derbyshire's methods. So, for music requiring short samples, the Fairlight would do the job in a fraction of the time. If we'd attempted the Derbyshire **Doctor Who** theme in 1981, a lot of it could have been done on the Fairlight.

But there was still a lot that couldn't. Anything needing longer samples, such as backgrounds and slow pieces, would still require the use of tape. So, as with many predictions, it didn't turn out quite as expected.

Nonetheless, the Fairlight offered many new facilities. I was particularly interested in its ability to merge two waveforms together and I still have morphed material from that time in my sound library. 'Mandochor' for instance, where the pluck of a mandolin evolves magically into a choir, or 'Combvox', a comb filtered waveform that turns into a baritone.

Yes, in 1981, we could still create sounds that nobody had heard before. The very same thing that had excited so many people back at the beginning of the Workshop.

A Change was Coming

It's easy now, with the benefit of hindsight, to imagine that we were all aware of approaching technical change, but our modus operandi remained much the same despite these one-off advances. The Fairlight CMI was not the catchall solution that the salesman had predicted, but a wonderful glimpse of what was to come. The variety of sounds at our disposal was becoming extensive, and the quality of taped sound impressive, but the equipment was large, and the use of it sometimes clumsy and mechanical. In those days, you needed a studio full of gear, and you really did need to play it all. But, in terms of technique, we were still closer to the old days than the brand new digital era.

We would imagine a sound, and search around the room for the right tools to bring it about. My lack of formal musical education, despite its disadvantages, made me less concerned about the received way to achieve things. There was more likelihood of producing innovative material, but the risks were that much greater, and we all walked a high wire between success and failure on a daily basis.

You could take almost any featured cue from a TV series as an example.

Let's look at this one.

A Long Way from Africa

I should have been here hours ago and this will take a while.

The commissionaire greets me as I walk through reception. One of the cheerier ones; a sadder version will replace him later on. The top corridor stretches out in front of me. DaVinci could have used this as practice for perspective drawing, because the doors at the far end are the size of my thumb. I trudge past the Radiophonic rooms to my left, and a little after Room 13 (Studio E) turn a sudden right. We are halfway down the length of the building, and this is the first opportunity to go right. We have now passed the back of the orchestral studio and can turn along its upper back wall. A short way along, we pass Malcolm Clarke's Studio C and suddenly, on the right, almost hanging over the chasm that runs along the far side of the building, we find Studio B. I'll be in here for a good twelve hours I expect.

It's a busy time, I'm in the middle of a nine-part series about Africa[21]. It will eventually amount to twenty-one reels of recorded tape. Ten and a half hours of material, comprising assembly, make up and final masters of the music[22]. The series first appears in the catalogue in July 1985, but the work extends across two to three months, and there are other projects running at the same time: a Radio 4 drama, work for BBC Plymouth, and short stings for TV Presentation[23].

The power switch is at the door, but only turns on a few of the many boxes of tricks. Most of them need switching on separately to avoid a surge. The room comes to life. Because it's hard for the gear to remember its settings overnight, I try to finish each piece in a day, unless it can be divided up into different tasks. Today, I'm hoping to score a sequence

---

[21] Dr. Ali Mazuri's **The Africans: A Triple Heritage**.
[22] Actual finished broadcast minutes will be much less. About 20 minutes for each of the nine programmes.
[23] TV Presentation is responsible for the voice links and trailers that occur between programmes.

in programme two of the series, covering the infamous Elmina Castle in Ghana. Thirty thousand slaves passed through this forbidding place until 1814, and were held in appalling conditions before being shipped across the Atlantic. The images are of the fort as it is now, cavernous damp spaces with little light. The soundtrack will simply have the commentary and music, so whatever I do will be exposed.

The sequence is about a minute and a half long, the image panning slowly around the rooms. It's clear that it requires a slow and measured feel and a sad and sombre atmosphere. At this moment, I have no idea how that will be achieved.

Surrounded by all this equipment, all these possibilities, a sort of frozen anxiety can take hold and inertia can set in, so something needs to happen fast.

Time to use the washing line technique. I lay down a constant string note for the duration of the sequence. I experiment with some chords, throwing them against this one string note. Various possibilities emerge, but this is such a harrowing scene, perhaps vocal sounds are necessary. However briefly, this will anchor the idea of a human presence between these walls, and might help with the writing of the piece. If it sounds right, then it might avoid the need for fancy footwork in the music.

Right from the early days, I've used my voice as a sound source. It's just another instrument in the room. Through a second door is the piano room. It's next to my studio, and so I can use it as an acoustic area. Perhaps just recording some low sung pitches might work, and then re-pitch them using tape speed control. But that would involve a lot of unknowns. A great deal of time would pass before knowing whether it was a good or bad idea. Luckily, there's another way.

A lot of us called it 'Tape Knitting', Robert Fripp may have invented it and called it 'Frippertronics', and I've coined the term 'Variable Feedback

Delay Loop'[24] but we are all referring to the same trick. It's best achieved using two reel-to-reel tape machines[25].

The left one's in record and the right one in playback. Sound that's recorded on the left has to travel right across to the machine on the right to be played back. This can be many seconds later[26]. It then feeds this back into machine one, where fresh material is still being recorded. The combination of new and old sound is then fed through the loop again. As you can imagine, it'll gradually build up the density of the sound and thicken the texture. One person can become a crowd. One cracking stick can become a whole forest. One pitched vocal note can become a choir. Success or failure becomes clear much sooner and time wouldn't be wasted.

I position the two tape machines and set them running. It plays the result back into headphones in the studio so I can vary my performance as it goes along. I start by humming a few notes that, after a few seconds, return to my headphones and I add more. The sound builds up, but it's a mess. Some sort of metronome would be useful. I could set up a synth to play a regular click which would be fed to my ears, but not be part of the recording, but something better occurs to me. If I clapped slowly and regularly, that sound would return and I could add to the claps. I try this. It sounds interesting, but very dry. I stop the recording and add some reverberation into the circuit; fairly short, room echo that simulates what we are seeing in the picture. I restart the recording. This sounds better. I'm clapping slowly and it's building up. After four or five passes around the loop, the clapping's full enough, and I'm tempted to start adding some humming. It seems right to scoop into the notes and not let them hold too long, and after a few passes there's a chorus of humming voices over the clapping. I let this run for a while. All the clapping and humming is returning over and over again, each time more textured and embedded

---
[24] It's a more descriptive term, that's useful to refer to in lectures.
[25] I have now managed to reproduce this in software.
[26] I found that it should be at least 7 seconds later, anything less just sounds like a repeating pattern and is less chaotic.

in the overall sound. I stop the machines and re-listen, this time with the picture. There's a rough commentary already on the film, provided by the director. What I've done is too busy once the commentary voice is added. I may have to re-record the whole thing, but it occurs to me that I could slow the recording down. Of course, back then, slowing would also reduce the pitch, but as yet I've not fixed a key for this music, so it should be fine. Reducing the speed has an immediate effect. All the effort put into the performance is stretched by the speed change. The clapping becomes more laborious and tired, and the humming becomes a richer and lower tone. There's a feeling of exhaustion and desperation in the sound.

I look at the time. It's already midnight. I need a break and find my way back to the long corridor. It's deserted. Any sessions in the other studios have finished, so it's quite possible that there are now only two people in this vast building. The commissionaire and me. I push open the double doors to reception and am aware of a strong smell of peppermints, and the sound of snoring. The commissionaire is lying across a bench behind the desk, so I'm on my own from now on.

I descend the centre stairs and visit the toilets. Not wanting to encounter sleeping beauty again, I return to the studio the back way.

This building wears a serious frown in the early hours. It's a grim path. The underlit void in the back of this vast shell has large creepy shadows and random metal stairways, platforms and tanks. The set of some dystopian movie. They do say there's a ghost down there, but I have never seen one. A ghost could hardly make me more uneasy.

I climb the stairs to my studio and close the door, aware that the scene I'm scoring is not likely to lift my spirits. Still, after a while, I forget the building, and immerse myself again in the project. All this seems so divorced from the programme it's to be part of, and light years away from the public who will watch it. There's a creative freedom here and now, but there will be a reckoning to come, when the director hears it and delivers his verdict.

It doesn't take too long to play serpentine chords that wind their way around the clapping and humming. Harmonic structure develops as I'm playing, and I go back to the held string note, rerecord it, and vary it according to the harmonies. The piece is working, and the writing's over. It just remains to mix the result into a useable recording and add it to the other cues already finished for the programme.

With the studio turned off and locked, I find my way back to Reception and the outside world. As I'm passing through, the telephone on the desk rings, and Mr Peppermint jumps awake. It's his boss in Broadcasting House, wondering why he hasn't been ringing in. As he splutters his excuses, I push through the outer door and head home.

Documentaries come in two flavours. Chronological and geographical.

The first stays in the same place, but moves through time; the second focuses on one subject in different locations. You need to have knowledge of music from different periods for the chronological programmes, and indigenous music for the geographical.

For that reason, this series on Africa was a steep learning curve. Each region of the continent has its own style of music. The northern and eastern sides are highly influenced by Muslim culture, but for the title sequence of the series, I did a lot of research into Ghanaian sounds.

Believe it or not, scores of African drumming do actually exist. I was lucky enough to track down a book of them in the Commonwealth Institute[27]. According to the preface, a Church of England priest,

---

[27] Sadly, this wonderful facility is no more and the institute only really exists online for public access, but in those days you could wander in off the street and use their library.

sent out to convert the natives of Ghana, became fascinated by their music. He was a musician himself, and had access to one of those early seismographs; a revolving cylinder which could record vibrations from earthquakes and aftershocks and transfer them onto paper. With a small amount of ingenuity, involving the addition of a sensitive pad alongside the machine, he made a graphical transcription of individual drummers. These players would come to him one at a time and 'play' their parts by drumming on the pad. He would then decipher the results, and render them in conventional score format. I'd been daunted by the prospect of writing music for a series about a place I'd never visited, and whose music I'd never considered, so this book was a great find.

I was allowed to borrow it for a week and took it back to Maida Vale to start realising his transcriptions.

Just one look at the score would tell you immediately that to manage this on a conventional sequencer or timeline would be tricky. But the Fairlight offered something special.

Although reduced to a common meter of 12/8, each individual part was playing against its neighbour, so that it was really a piece in 2/4, 4/4, 3/4 and 6/8 simultaneously. With no barlines, and with different tempos and meters on every track, the Fairlight was an exciting place to experiment. Its composer page allowed you enormous freedom.

Transferring all the printed notation into the machine was a lengthy job, and the results only emerged after a period. Unlike western pop and rock, where the constant beat mainly comes from the bass drum, this African music relied on the agogo bell and clapping as its reference, allowing free rein for all the drumming parts below. After a full day of data entry, I was able to see how it all fitted together. I found listening to the result surprisingly emotional. I was rediscovering long forgotten sounds, tapped onto that seismograph over a century earlier.

Drawing on the music from an entire continent was exhilarating. I became fascinated by the 'Kora', an instrument from West Africa. It comprises a large gourd as the resonator, which is held close to the player, with a long fretboard extending outwards into the room. I say fretboard, but there are no frets. The twenty-one strings, divided into a row for the left and right hand, are played with their open tunings; the highest strings being furthest from the player. The tunings allow for a scale to be achieved by alternating the left and right rows. The thumbs are often dealing with the bass and the index fingers with the top. The rest of the hand is grasping onto two handles which hold the instrument in position. It is different in every respect from anything that Western music has to offer, and is proof, if any were needed, that the interface between player and instrument is crucial in shaping the sound it makes. Even today, in our concerts, it's essential to use the right controller for each type of performance. Keyboard, Guitar with MIDI control, Wind Controller, and a button matrix interface are all used at different times.

The Kora was to feature in a number of cues in the series, and I rooted around to see if there might be a musician from the UK who could play for me. There was no one, and so I reluctantly started to look at recorded samples of the instrument. The National Sound Archive had a large collection of world music, and at the time was situated at the top of Exhibition Road in London. By chance, on the day that I rang them, they had just arranged a visit of a world renowned Kora player from Senegal. After some delicate negotiations, I got permission to go to the Archive and record him playing some indigenous music to use in the series. It was a fascinating experience. His thumbs and fingers were so dextrous, it was hard to see how he was conjuring such a wonderful sound from the instrument. There was something really satisfying using that music embedded into my own[28]. It was a way of accommodating the needs of incidental music whilst staying true to the original music of the region.

---

[28] To be clear, his performance was complete and my contribution added. He and I were credited on those cues.

I was always struck by the confidence that directors had in us. Because of our reputation for innovation, they assumed that we could turn our hand to anything. We were seen as a progressive department, constantly looking for ways to achieve previously unheard sounds, straining our necks over the horizon to see what was coming next. That's not a stance you can keep up forever; occasionally you have to settle back and enjoy the progress you've made. The tally of projects from 1983 to 1986 shows a relentless stream of work. The composers and their equipment were becoming a well-oiled machine

Horizon: Mathematics	August 1984	TV Science Features	BBC2	Incidental Music
Lift Off	January 1985	TV Children	BBC1	Sig/Jingles
D-Day to Berlin	March 1985	Current Affairs	BBC1	Signature
Brazil	May 1985	TV Continuing Education	BBC2	Signature Tune
Autumn Promotions	August 1985	TV Presentation	BBC2	Jingle
The Big Novel	October 1985	Drama	Radio 4	Signature Tune
Christmas Jingle 1985	November 1985	TV Presentation	BBC1	Jingle
Double Image	November 1985	Drama Plays	BBC1	Incidental Music
The Bridge at Orbigo	March 1986	Drama	Radio 3	Incidental Music
Choices 1986	May 1986	MP02	BBC1	Signature Tune
Talking Business	June 1986	TV Continuing Education	BBC	Signature Tune & Incidental
Children of Green Knowe	June 1986	TV Children	BBC1	Signature Tune & Incidental

During this period, there was never a shortage of work, and run of the mill music rubbed shoulders with shows that would be remembered long after. **The Children of Green Knowe** was a memorable project. It was an excellent adaptation of the book, strong on atmosphere and with some exceptional performances, and a gift for a composer.

I decided to use violin, oboe and harp at the title and incidental sessions, and add my own lines in the studio.

Writing for some instruments is so specialised that the only way to have confidence in your score, ahead of a session, is to speak to the player. You need to discuss the limitations of the instrument and the playing technique, and after composing the music, send the score to the musician to iron out any last minute problems. So when time is money during the session, you can concentrate on the performance, rather than patching up an ill-written part. The harp was one such instrument. Looking at many old paintings, you'd think it was a simple instrument, but a modern concert harp is complex. It has twelve pedals, so that it can play in any key, so a bipedal harpist has their work cut out.

After consulting the player and adjusting the score accordingly, the day of the session arrived.

As we rehearsed the title music, it became clear that there had been one point I hadn't discussed in enough depth: the tempo. The players were not performing to a metronome beat or any other instrumentation from the tape, but simply playing live onto the recording. To keep some semblance of order, I'd decided to do some primitive conducting. After my problems with the original *Space for Man* session, this was rash. The harp part was working well, and I was delighted to hear it sound the way I'd imagined, but it was too slow. I conducted faster, but to my surprise it didn't speed up. The violist and oboist had sensibly decided to ignore my gesticulations and follow the harp, which doggedly stuck to its original tempo.

I'd written something that was not possible to play any faster, but it was sounding so good, it would have been stupid not to accept it as it was. Perhaps I could figure out a way to get it to last the right amount of time to fit the title sequence.

After the session, back in my studio, I reached for the tape speed control. Of course, this not only increased the tempo but also raised the pitch. So now, if you listen to the broadcast titles of **The Children of Green Knowe**, the instruments have a quaint music box feel. It's over the picture of a rocking horse, and it seems intentional, but it was pure serendipity.

This series was a magical time for all of us who worked on it. Its magic still works for me today. There are occasions when there's such strength in the narrative of a story, it writes the music for you, and you seem to be a conduit. A few similar experiences have happened since, especially whilst writing music for the band. It's what keeps you going.

Green Knowe was so enjoyable that when Colin Cant the director was looking for a composer for his next project, he gave me a ring. In many ways **Moondial** was uncannily similar in mood to **Green Knowe**, and I hesitated to accept the job. I knew that however hard I tried, I wouldn't be able to deliver the same level of work. Such an intense experience has to be a one off. It was with a lot of regret that I turned it down. To hardened professional composers, this must seem like pure folly, but I'd become so immersed in **The Children of Green Knowe** that it felt like a betrayal to do something so similar soon afterwards.

That show was to mark the end of an era. If the history of the Radiophonic Workshop was a three act play, and the original pioneers saw us through Act One, and multitrack and polyphonic synthesisers had helped us through the second act, then at this point we stood teetering on the brink of the final act of the drama: the digital age.

Part 3

Embarrassed with Riches

Market Forces

Over the years, I've scored a lot of **Horizon** programmes. They've given me a small amount of knowledge of a great many subjects. Get me talking at a party, and I could give the impression that I know about Eclipses, Parkinson's Disease, the Japanese Bullet Train, Human Parasites, and many others. On this occasion, the subject was Easter Island.

The director had brought an anthropologist along for some expert input. He was a serious man. His voice, his clothes, his hair; there wasn't a bone in his body that wasn't serious[1].

"In programmes about places," I said, "it's often useful to write music that might have been played at the time. What would that have been?"

He nodded slowly. "Oh yes, they would have made music."

"And what sort of instruments would they use?"

"Ah," he said with some enthusiasm. "They banged stones on the earth."

"Seriously?"

"Oh, yes."

After they had left, I spent a few minutes staring into space, wondering whether I was expected to score the whole programme using stones. It was especially worrying, because the BBC had paved over any earth that it owned in Maida Vale, and I might have been forced to work from home. I gave the director a ring.

"Forget the indigenous music," he said. "Go for electronics."

---

[1] Well there was, but I'll allow you to work that one out.

Electronic music has no associations; it can work in all manner of contexts, far removed from scifi. If you visualise someone playing the cello, however wonderful the music, it just doesn't work with the picture of a wild animal. Sometimes you need to hear the sound, and not imagine who's playing it.

I'm glad to say that when I worked on **Horizon**, it assumed its audience was intelligent and didn't feel the need to over emphasise. These days, some documentaries have to try a lot harder to keep the viewers engaged. For the first two-thirds of the programme, they convince us that the world's going to end, then start the last third with…

"You think that's bad, wait till you hear this!"

Mind you, I could say the same thing about my attempt at the **Horizon** title music.

They wanted an update of their iconic opening, written by Wilfred Josephs for the series launch in 1964. The Workshop was well stocked with gear, and we were well liked by programme makers, and so we felt that we could undertake almost anything that dropped on our desks. Digital methods were clearly going to impact us sooner or later, but for now we were a touch complacent, riding on the mid eighties boom.

For the **Horizon** remake, I got far too pre-occupied with the Fairlight. It was still fairly new, and the temptation to achieve the whole piece on it was too much to bear. To make matters worse, I chose to use my own voice samples, unrelieved by any other sound.

The graphic artist was also having a bad day at the office. She had decided to have the whole sequence rendered in grey, and even stranger, to show the title 'Horizon' at the beginning.

As I've said, this was an era of 'can do' and we set about it with unreasonable enthusiasm.

After a couple of weeks, the piece was duly completed and hit the airways a month later.

You might find a copy of it on YouTube, but I can't imagine why.

For me, the whole experience proved, without a shadow of a doubt, that colour's a good thing, and titles should always be at the end. Using the little amount of available digital gear just for the sake of it had not paid off. We couldn't continue operating in a vacuum. Sooner or later we would have to open our eyes to progress being made in the industry at large.

The BBC had always prided itself on being self sufficient. It had buildings all over west London and could mount productions with no outside assistance. The term 'out sourcing' was hardly ever heard. Apart from project-based requirements, such as specialised props or costumes, the Corporation could sail from one production to another, knowing that Auntie Knew Best. The Workshop had, from its inception, occupied a niche in the audio industry, producing tailor made sound and music for BBC Radio and Television. It was held in high regard by many other electronic music studios because of its early pioneering days, and despite our bread-and-butter work, still regarded us as something special..

The composers at the Workshop though were more apprehensive. Technological advances had given us an amazing array of possibilities. It became one of the exciting parts of the job. But unlike the old days, when sounds were homegrown in the department, these came from equipment bought on the open market. A market accessible to any aspiring composer with funds.

Our association with more conventional scores led to a comparison with these new composers outside the BBC. We found ourselves with two objectives. To turn in original electro-acoustic sound and music as we'd always done, but also compete with professional media composers writing traditional scores. Their world was changing with the popularisation of new technology and, in a strange turn around, we had to be in step with them.

The Corporation, in 1985, was a massive collection of interconnected equipment which didn't take kindly to having a new kid on the block. Any change had to be fed through the entire network with enormous care, because the BBC was not something you could turn off whilst you did the maintenance. For that reason, many engineering updates, including the arrival of stereo and colour television, sat later on the timeline than you'd imagine.

But the day dawned when we had to face the fact that with the advent of digital audio recording at broadcast quality, our world would change for good.

The 'analogue' method of reproduction that had gone before used a blanket system of capture. A camera would open its shutter and allow the light to spill across the film and plant the image of a scene. A recording head on an analogue tape recorder would fire the sound from a microphone across a moving tape of iron filings which would reproduce an image of the sound waves.

'Digital' approaches reproduction completely differently. It will analyse every tiny change in a waveform and reduce it to a very fast and long stream of binary 'digits'. Each of these are either on or off, but when reconstituted or played back, will re-assemble themselves and play a sound that's a faithful rendition of the original.

This is as different a world as electric cars are to their petrol predecessors. Many of us can remember switching from cassettes to mp3 players. That moment represented the change for consumers from analogue to digital, and it gave us better quality, and machines that were easier to use[2]. We took it in our stride.

On a professional level though, this was a seismic event.

It had been the most wonderful journey. Rather like the composer who can trace his creative ancestry back centuries in an unbroken line, we too felt connected to the early discoveries in audio. The history of sound recording was one of constant improvement, where each step brought up challenges for the next generation, that were duly solved and passed on. We were proud of the quality we achieved.

So, being told that the next step would be total renewal came as a shock. The long line of analogue development, with all its notable successes, was to end, and be replaced by digital technology.

I now realised what the original pioneers had experienced with the arrival of voltage-controlled synthesis. Our way of work was being upended by an unstoppable force. By this time though, the influence of manufacturers outside the BBC was commonplace, and their enthusiasm for new technology in the musical arena was taking off. So yes, we did feel daunted by this new age, but we looked forward to what it might bring[3]. The engineers heralded it as a genuine replacement for everything that had gone before.

This was not the case. Well, not for us. Digital and Analogue were like the Montagues and Capulets[4]. You couldn't be in both, you had to choose sides. And yet if your work stayed in the digital domain, a lot of creative possibilities were absent.

---

[2] Why is it that I still see cassette tape wound round the central reservations on motorways? Some drivers appear to be making the change one tape at a time!
[3] I must admit that, having grappled with intrusive tape hiss for decades, I was certainly pleased to be relieved of that.
[4] Well, no they weren't, but there's an analogy there somewhere.

It was not a replacement of everything that had gone before, but an immaculate way to record audio and alter its level. Little more. It would take a good while before manipulation of the sound would be possible. There was no phasing effect, no ring modulation, no reversing sound, no speed change, and so the list went on. Since we spent most of our time changing and manipulating sound, we had a problem.

The new technology had arrived, allowing us to do things we'd only dreamt of, but also denying us the ability to continue with the things we took for granted. We felt as if we were boarding an unmoored boat, with one foot on the deck and one on the jetty. Doing the splits, trying to keep our act together.

We had to compromise, starting work in the analogue domain and passing the resulting product through a digital stage to master it. Its delivery might have been in bright new shiny digital, but we'd assembled it using all the old techniques.

Anyone trying to write an accurate history of this period is faced with a dilemma. The presence of digital gear in a studio didn't mean that the whole audio path was digital, and it can be confusing to construct a definitive timeline. So although I have mentioned digital recording first and MIDI second, the two jostled for position in the early eighties, and it depended on each individual studio as to how connected they were.

For us though, MIDI had a more profound effect on the actual creation of sound and music than digital recording. Individual pieces of digital gear, such as the Fairlight, and the Roland Samplers were already being used, but were standalone and not connected to anything else. It wasn't until the gear communicated with MIDI that things really took off.

The Musical Instrument Digital Interface, to use its full title, was one of digital's great successes. It provided some much-needed control, but was an entirely new experience. Embedding it into our pattern of work was going to be hard, if only because it reduced the multiple boxes of tricks in our studios, and forced us to concentrate on smaller but cleverer ones.

Our creative lives till then had been without boundaries. We were dealing with real sounds and real time performances, our stage was unrestricted. Now it was marked up before we started. Every note was measured, every tempo constant, every sound predetermined[5]. True, all these things were capable of change, but not without that extra moment of decision.

Why was it necessary for one instrument to talk to another? Instruments had hitherto been happy just to be themselves, without the need to speak in tongues. Previously, if you felt that a sound wasn't right, you'd alter it by adjusting the device that made it. Now you had to send it a message. It was the difference between getting up and shutting the window, and writing a note to another person asking them to shut it. There was now another tier of decision making, and it felt more like a restriction than a liberation. Our synthesisers had memorised settings for a while now, but within the confines of each instrument. MIDI was a universal language which meant that the settings for a whole piece, eventually for a whole studio, could be memorised in one place.

MIDI doesn't care if it passes through an instrument, a sequencer, a mixer, a computer, a lighting rig, a control surface, a foot pedal or whatever; its language remains the same, and any of those devices can take what they need from it, and ignore the rest.

It was a fundamental shift in the way that we viewed our technical environment. When I've talked about 'playing the studio', I've been referring to separate pieces of gear, each with its own character, a large bulky collection of instruments that were physically occupying space. Now the so-called instruments, or sources of sound, were not in front of us when we played. They had disappeared altogether, or at the very least

---

[5] Live spontaneous performance was possible but only by abandoning the barlines and the metre.

become so reduced in size, they were consigned to a rack out of sight.

Rick Wakeman must have hated the arrival of MIDI. His iconic nest of synthesiser keyboards on stage with the band Yes was his calling card. We all marvelled at the way he could dart from one to another in the middle of a song, playing impossible riffs, standing up one moment, sitting the next, only head and shoulders visible behind this array of gear. The reason he found this necessary, was a lack of communication between one piece of equipment and another. With MIDI, all that changed, and his stage rig looked like a period piece. Now, one keyboard could control and play many other devices.

It's a testament to the original designers[6] of MIDI that, strictly speaking, we are still on Version 1[7]. Although there have been additions to its scope over the years, they've not involved a rewriting of the original platform. Right from the start, they had left plenty of space for development. If only a few other innovations had been so thorough. Imagine, for instance, if there had only been one sample rate for digital recording, what a relief that would have been. Instead, we constantly chastise ourselves for starting a new project at the wrong rate[8]. With MIDI, that initial learning curve has value today. Even the music software that we use and take for granted on our computers uses MIDI as its internal language[9].

As with all innovations, there were consequences. We now had the ability to produce music quickly and reliably, but that resulted in directors assuming that they could get more for their money. Thanks to MIDI, we

---

[6] Dave Smith, founder of the early synthesiser company Sequential Circuits saw the need for a protocol that would link devices together and released the first version of the MIDI standard in 1983.

[7] In fact, only recently has Version 2 been announced, and at the time of writing has not yet been finalised.

[8] I worked with one composer who had started so many projects at the wrong rate, he stuck a gigantic poster to the wall reading 'For the Love of God. 48k'.

[9] Open Sound Control (OSC) is another language used to communicate between devices. It's often used these days in live settings for music but also lighting and other stage cueing.

were becoming more of a production line.

The ability of one keyboard to speak to another seemed rather ridiculous at first, but then other devices appeared, such as synths without keyboards[10]. So, there was now a need for a dummy keyboard to control the synths. Next to arrive was the MIDI sequencer[11]. Sequencers were part of early electronic music gear, but their capacity was limited. The Synthi 100 had a large sequencer, but even that would only play a total of two hundred and fifty-six notes. MIDI could offer a great deal more.

Take the QX1, for example. It seemed to encapsulate the wonderful and the absurd under one roof. It was a desktop device about the size of a small writing desk, capable of recording your live performance from the dummy keyboard and playing an ensemble of synthesisers attached to its output. But once the data was in there, you were faced with one of the most infuriating interfaces ever encountered.

It was surreal. Imagine being outside your front door. Inside your house, in a back room, is a band of musicians. You need to get them to play, but the only way to achieve this is to employ the services of a runner. He will rush to and fro, from the front door to the back room, with your musical instructions. Oh, and the only way you can speak to him is through the letterbox, and he only understands note names and numbers. Oh, and you can only tell him about one note at a time.

You get the picture. We were used to selecting equipment from around the room—to stare laboriously at a tiny slit of a display and enter numerical descriptions of our music all day seemed absurd. It was as if we'd suffered some sort of accident. How on earth could anyone work like this?

It was clear that we needed some encouragement to embrace this technology and when a post became vacant, the head of the Workshop,

---

[10] Especially the Yamaha TX816, a whole rack of synthesisers that were in essence eight DX7s.
[11] A device that plays back musical instructions over time.

Brian Hodgson, decided to spread the net wider than usual and advertised outside the Corporation[12].

Richard Attree was the last composer employed by the Radiophonic Workshop, and had been working with MIDI before he joined. In fact, he had been working with the QX1.

Imagine the QX1 as a swimming pool[13]. Here we were toiling up and down, thrashing through the water, wondering why we seem to be going slower and slower, when this Olympian joins us. His dive is so extensive and effortless that he's halfway down the pool before he takes a stroke. His turns are smooth and instant, and when it's time to leave the pool, he walks on the water to get out. Richard's skill with this MIDI device was impressive, and he wrote many effective pieces using it. He made it look so easy. This new skill set was a much needed boost for the Workshop and came at precisely the right moment.

When it came to composing modern competitive music[14], Richard's style of composition, and his meticulous attitude to mixing and production, kept us on our toes. I found it daunting and exciting in equal measure. Before his arrival, I was in severe danger of missing the bus, but his contribution[15] kept me on board, even if, at times, I was holding on by my fingernails, with my coat tails flying.

In January 1984, Apple had launched its desktop computer, and by August 1986, Brian Hodgson had arrange to purchase two Apple Mac Plus computers for us. No letterbox screen here. This screen was massive, about the size of a DVD case. Well, it seemed big to us. In addition, it

---

[12] Brian had had been away from the BBC between 1972 and 1977 and could see the value of looking further afield.
[13] It's a stretch, but bear with me.
[14] Directors were now less attracted to the avant-garde, and more in need of contemporary music.
[15] The Radio 1 Programme *The Dream*, which featured his music throughout, won the Sony Gold Award for the most creative use of Radio in 1989.

introduced the world to object-oriented programming and the possibility of having folders and files, and a desktop. And there was the mouse. Looking at a screen and moving a cursor with your right hand on the desk was very odd, but surprisingly intuitive.

It seems strange now that the QX1 sequencer could have lasted a second with an Apple Mac as competition, but the QX1 was a dedicated piece of gear. There was a prevailing attitude that equipment should be a master of one specific task. There was no place for a jack of all trades in a professional environment; it was as stupid as expecting a hammer to do the job of a screwdriver. This was a fact of life. We hadn't ever experienced a device that was good at almost anything. The BBC's engineering establishment was quite conservative and took some persuading when it came to such things; they did use early computers, but strictly green screen and not a mouse in sight. Everything entered on a command line.

The Workshop had been using the BBC Micro since its inception in 1981, but this was a tiny forerunner of what was to come, and although we used it to find cue points in a stream of timecode for synchronising purposes, its small memory couldn't multitask[16].

Everyone will tell you that a computer's only as good as its software, and the early incarnations of music software were basic[17]. You still had lists of MIDI note values similar to the QX1, but these were scrollable lists, and cutting, copying, and pasting of data was easy. Despite all this, we knew that this was only a tiny taste of what was to come.

One of the obvious advantages of this brave new world was the ability to memorise what you had done, without committing it to a recording. We'd hitherto been knitting the jumpers[18], when now we only had to

---

[16] This was a system called *Syncwriter*. A joint effort by Ray White (hardware) and Jonathan Gibbs (software). It worked well because its use was so specific.
[17] We used *Performer* software to start with.
[18] I did warn you about the metaphors in my introduction. You only have yourself to blame.

write the instructions for the machine that knitted them. Making the jumper could happen later, whenever convenient. But there were still many things that had to be done using the old ways. The new MIDI gear wouldn't handle longer sections of audio, these had to be manipulated in the studio as before. It would take a while for that to change. But there would come a time when the physical tools in the room would give way to a virtual world of timelines and plugins and our entire working life would collapse into a box. Leaving us to rummage around in its limitless interior to pull out ideas in any tangible form.

The digital revolution didn't happen in a day. It wasn't a coup. Along the way, various new machines would appear and we were always keen to test them. After all, new and original material was our USP[19]. I do wonder though whether I should have volunteered so often to work at the USP coalface. I was the 'go-to guinea pig', the guy who couldn't say 'no'.

There was the ADAT eight track machine, for instance. It was going to be used on an adaptation of *Pilgrims Progress* for the World Service. The ADAT format was a dedicated digital recording system that's still used today. This incarnation, though, was a rather traditional design. Traditional in the sense of being a recognisable multitrack tape recorder and not an 'in the box' computer. This particular model boasted a tape deck[20] that would heal itself if scratched. I remember the rep from the distributor making a particular point of it, as if it was what we'd all been waiting for.

What he failed to mention was the machine's reluctance to rewind. It became worse as it heated up. You'd press the rewind button, and it would creep to the left, sometimes lurching for a moment to give you hope, but never getting anywhere fast. In the end, I resorted to cranking the spools around with my fist.

---

[19] Unique Selling Point.
[20] The surface on which the tape revolved.

This was a long production, with a lot for me to contribute, but the malicious machine was hell bent on stopping me. I saw now why it had a self-healing surface, and wondered how fast it would deal with repeated blows from a chisel.

The industry's laboured attempts to make sense of this new world made your head spin.

Some time away was called for.

Outside the Box

The BBC felt, quite rightly, that after fifteen years' work for the Corporation, you needed some time off, and encouraged you to take a sabbatical. A gracious gesture that many staff welcomed. At any given moment, there would always be employees circumnavigating the globe like satellites, trying to experience the world, before the BBC took them back into its bosom for the rest of their working lives. I decided against travel. Airports are hideous places, and besides, there was something else of interest. In my early days, before I joined the BBC, I'd been involved in acting and rather liked the idea of treading the boards again. I signed up to a six-week summer school in Islington.

The experience proved valuable in a lot of ways, some of them far removed from the theatre.

I'd become increasingly irritated by the casual way that electronic studios were thrown together. They were constrained by the dimensions of the gear in them. There was always an ongoing battle between looking straight ahead across a mixing desk to the speakers beyond, and having to swivel to the right or left to play a synthesiser keyboard or operate other sound making gear, taking you off axis with the speakers.

When you spend some time away from something, it gives you a genuine opportunity to focus on its deficiencies, and so when I returned from my sabbatical, I'd worked out a way of improving studio design. Brian Hodgson, like me, was always excited to try new ideas, and was encouraged to see what I was planning.

It was pure coincidence, but around that time Yamaha had developed a new digital mixer, the DMP7. Its early reviews were mixed. Some had criticised it for having a lot of noise on its output caused by poor analogue to digital converters, and they regarded it as a good stab at the new world of digital, but only that. For me though, they would play a vital role in this proposed new studio. I was suggesting the use of seven DMP7s. Five mixing the output of various sound sources around the room, and two closer to the front that would act as group and master faders. Because each of these mixers was a neat eight channel device, they could easily sit beneath the gear that they were mixing, without disturbing the view to the speakers. This needed to be a studio for a composer.

For that, he or she would need equal access to a MIDI keyboard, a computer QWERTY keyboard, a computer screen, a mixer, a TV monitor and, of course, stereo speakers. A tall order. A lot of this was achieved by using layering at different heights; the keyboard, the lowest, the computer keyboard above, the screen above that, the TV monitor higher than that, with the stereo speakers either side. The two DMP7 mixers serving as groups and masters were positioned on the higher level, slightly to the right. The other five mixers sat on the lower level beneath short racks which contained the outboard gear (rack mounted synthesisers and effects, as well as a digital recorder). All this had to sit in some custom built joinery, so we had to decide how big this thing was going to be. The furniture would have to be a horseshoe shape, with the composer sitting in the middle, reaching out around the studio to operate the mixers below the gear. And so, the very first event on the long road to producing this new studio took place one Monday morning. I sat on a typist's chair with my arms outstretched, whilst Brian Hodgson wielded a tape measure. By adding the depth of the mixers and the approximate depth of the rack mounted gear above, we arrived at a suggested circumference for this horseshoe.

No one knew if this enterprise would work or not. So we decided to build a mockup of the studio. We asked the BBC carpenters to make us the U-shaped surface out of plywood, which we then rested on filing cabinets.

By a stroke of luck the measurement we'd arrived at, turned out to be just a few inches shorter than John Baker's old room, Room 11. This was not being used, and so we built the mock up in there, and allowed the rest of the Workshop to run as normal.

Our engineers were understandably dubious about the whole venture. We were suggesting feeding the output of five mixers that had been slated as being too hissy, into two other mixers with the same unfavourable reviews. They predicted an audio snowstorm and a very unprofessional result. There was only one way to find out, and so with the very willing cooperation of Yamaha, who lent us seven DMP7s, the whole experiment got under way.

It was a lengthy process. Over the next few months, we added infrastructure and gear to the studio, until the viability of the idea became clear. The mixers were not only digital, but also had motorised faders and were controllable from elsewhere. So, a computer could tell the mixers which preset to choose, and how to configure all the controls. When I say computer, we are talking early Mac here. One of the programmes on Mac computers then was a programming language called *Hypercard*. With this, we could put together a piece of custom software to act as overall control of the studio. With seven DMP7 mixers, it would be ridiculous to have to reset each one to a new patch or configuration, so some sort of software command centre was essential. Thus, we could greatly reduce that problem of hiss, so feared by the engineers. Because only those faders delivering sound were left open and hiss from all the others faded out. Oddly, the studio never suffered from the hiss problem, and if you listen back to the countless pieces of music produced in the round studios, there's a clarity and cleanness to the sound.

I was now using John Baker's old room as my place of work. A hot and sweaty experience. When showing directors into the room, I felt rather like a kid with a new train set. All very impressive, but nowhere to stand. The director would sit uncomfortably behind me, reversing out of the open end of the horseshoe, with his back squeezed against the corridor wall. Still, they were all very amenable, and more than willing to take part in the experiment.

The time was fast approaching when we had to decide whether this had been a success, and whether we wanted to build a studio for real in one of the main composing areas of the Workshop. What happened next was flattering, but also a surprise. Elizabeth Parker had really taken to this circular solution, and since her room was up for refurbishment, it was she who had the first round studio, not me. After so much work designing and testing it, I was still going to be shut in Room 11 with the prototype. In fact, in the long run it turned out to be a good idea. When the installation started in my old area of Studio B, it took much less time to construct, because so many early problems had been solved during the first build. So finally, with my studio complete, I could reap the benefits of that idea I'd had during my three months away from the BBC.

The Director General was invited to the official opening of Elizabeth's studio. Not as slick an event as we'd hoped. The triggering of the opening piece of music which ushered us into the horseshoe failed to start, and the cake tasted of onions. We discovered afterwards that the carefully baked cake in the shape of the studio was not to blame, but it was the knife they had given us to cut it that brought tears to our eyes.

With my studio completed, it seemed like a good idea to have another stab at a proper opening, and invitations were sent out to the press and various guests from the BBC. To show off the futuristic side of the design, we attached small white dots to the faders of all seven mixers, and wrote a piece of music, in fact simply a line of instructions, that would control them all. With the light from an ultraviolet bulb in the ceiling above the horseshoe, the effect was dramatic. For people who had no experience of motorised faders at all, the sight of 70 of them doing a slow Mexican wave around the studio was rather impressive. It certainly spiced up many of the press reviews, all of which were encouraging. In fact, we were the cover article in *Sound on Sound* magazine in February 1989.

Our two circular studios were a turning point. It was the first time that the new digital age had been allowed to shape not just the quality of the audio, but also the fundamental way that a studio functioned. These days, centralising control over a studio is commonplace, and the horseshoe layout is just taken for granted. It's now so much easier to design spaces when the equipment's neater, but at the time it was an innovation on several levels. For years, the Workshop had rather revelled in the idea of the makeshift studio, with its hastily plugged gear and hit and miss results. We thought of ourselves as 'tinkering in the loft', daring to connect unlikely devices together just to see what happened, and being the first to do so. In fact, this is still part of our image to this day, but around that time, we were expected to deliver more material and quicker, and we needed the luxury of an easier life.

Bangor

Or Is It?

It's in our itinerary as Bangor. It's on the setlist as Bangor. But Bangor it most certainly is not.

If it was Bangor, we would have turned right back there, but we turned left. It's pitch dark, but I know my right from my left. No, we are going to Pwllheli. Pwllheli. Is that so hard? Well, yes… it's got far too many consonants[21].

In fact, it's only a few miles away from Portmeirion, where we played our very first concert as a touring band in 2013.

This time, rather than a rock festival, it's a whole weekend dedicated to SciFi and Fantasy; billed as 'Scifi Weekender 2018'.

We roll up around 9pm. This is a holiday camp that's been taken over to stage the event. All the holiday homes (basically posh static caravans) are

---

[21] Apologies to our Welsh readers.

available to use, and they've booked us in to one of them for two nights. There are nine of us, with two more to arrive the next day, so there must be some mistake. The caravan sleeps six, and only then if they've stepped out of a C.S. Lowry painting. My matchstick figure has long since disappeared.

Neil, our unflappable tour manager, phones back to reception to explain the problem.

"Ah," said the sleepy voice on the other end. "*You must talk to Jack. It's no good me giving you his number, he's turned his phone off. Perhaps you'd better go down to the Void and find him. He's easy to spot, he's dressed as The Joker.*"

The event has already started and there is a fancy dress party in full swing. Neil and Mark go back to the office to sort things out and, after a great deal of discussion, we end up with three caravans spread out all across the site. Paddy, Roger, and myself share one of them, and unpack.

The next morning we set out to look at the venue, in preparation for the evening's concert. Five Stormtroopers on roller skates overtake us as we cross a small bridge into the main thoroughfare. A child dwarfed by a lightsaber clings onto his dad dressed as Gandalf as they open the door to Starbucks, and two attractive young ladies pass by on stilts. They are not wearing character costumes, just leotards, but nobody is complaining.

We tell the security guard we're here to look at the venue and enter the gloom of 'The Main Void'. Down on the stage, two warriors from a computer game are playing out a scene in front of a gigantic video screen[22]. It's only 10 o'clock in the morning and there's already a packed house.

Every concert's preceded by a sound check. A chance to assemble the

---

[22] In fact, a vast array of individual pixels made up of 160 panels wired together across the back.

gear, plug up the yards of wire, and see if it all works.

But this comes after three or four days in a rehearsal studio in High Wycombe, to the west of London. No drums, just us and the gear. We're as quiet as mice, all listening on earphones, just as we do in a concert. So it's easy to imagine that this enclosed audio world is all there is, until you arrive at the next venue and realise that, yet again, you'll have to make contact.

The search for extraterrestrial life commences, and lines are laid between us and this other world. It feels alien and unnerving every time, but there's one thing that grounds us. 'Lightness'[23]. Zoe Martin, our front of house engineer, uses the same track at every venue as her reference. It tells her how the acoustic of this venue differs from the others and what needs to be done to fix our sound as it travels outwards to the audience. We hear that song and know that 'Zoe's in the house'. All will be well.

We get allocated a dressing room and despite the security guard's best efforts at keeping us out of the building in case we were up to no good, we finally troop on stage. This is an appreciative audience, but not typical. We're not the only thing they came to see. There are countless other attractions, so we're just the next significant thing in a long line of significant things, but we are well received. One number which we premiered in Bluedot the previous year has suddenly become topical. Stephen Hawking died just a week before this concert, and he contributed to a piece called 'We Would Not Be Here'. As I introduce it, and mention his input, it's clear how popular he is with this scifi crowd, and how much he's missed. A world-renowned scientist who inspired and excited everyone.

This gig's a revelation to me. I've not properly understood how these themed weekends work till now. Quite simply, it is four days of complete escapism and fun from beginning to end. I have never see so many people

---

[23] By Death Cab for Cutie, from their album *Transatlanticism* (2003).

of all ages enjoying themselves like this. The weekend revolves around Cosplay[24], and competitions are held to pick the most accurate portrayals. For one poor guy though, the weekend has not gone as planned.

I first spot him outside the rear entrance to the venue. Five others are waiting to get called onto the stage; they are well turned out, but he has decided to go all out for the big prize, and has turned up as the creature from the **Alien** movies. His costume is so convincing that it genuinely spooks me. The person inside is invisible, and all you can see is this overhanging head with multiple jaws lolling out of a shiny black carcass. A seven foot patent leather beetle.

But he doesn't win.

The head was already hanging; it must have switched from horror to pathos in a split second. At this moment, he must be looking for a suitable hole in the costume through which to pour vast quantities of alcohol.

But he has the right idea. What really interests audiences are blockbuster stories. **Alien**, **Star Wars**, **Doctor Who**; they're certain to attract a mass following.

Similarly, we've always been on the lookout for big subjects. And what could be bigger than the Apocalypse[25]?

Big Stories

| A Woman's Story (Annie Besant) | April 1988 | South & East TV | BBC1 | Incidental |

---

[24] I would be criticised for calling this fancy dress; this is taken a lot more seriously, and involves very accurate portrayals of characters from scifi or fantasy.
[25] Having been on **The One Show**, I know how to pull off tenuous links!

Bluebeard's Castle	May 1989	Music and Arts TV	BBC2	FX
Natural World: Owls	May 1988	Natural History Unit	BBC2	Incidental
The Great Rift	May 1988	Natural History Unit	BBC2	Title & Incidental
Almeida Festival	June 1988	Music and Arts TV	BBC2	Signature Tune
Nursery Crimes: Tom Thumb	August 1988	TV Feats Bristol	BBC1	Incidental
Open Air	August 1988	General Features Manchester	BBC1	Signature Tune
Revelation	October 1988	Religious Broadcasting	Radio 4	Incidental

The Book of Revelation had never struck me as ripe for adaption. It could never be a franchise[26]. Nevertheless, a religious department producer contacted the Workshop. He wanted to create a version for Radio 4.

This was a one-off pet project that slipped under the radar of programme controllers, and magically got a budget.

In 1988, with the outside world threatening to overtake us, these complete programmes remained viable for the Workshop. Because of their complexity, they took a long time to produce, but nobody was standing over us with a stopwatch recording the number of broadcast minutes we achieved each day. Outside the BBC, it would have cost far too much.

I still had the reputation as the person you should ask to do anything

---

[26] *Revelation 2* would be out of the question.

that was a one off, was a bit weird, and would probably take longer and involve a lot more grief than anyone else was prepared to put up with. My catalogue's strewn with special projects like these, but I'm not complaining, because one of them is the **Doctor Who** title music, and that's become the best calling card anyone could have wished for.

Besides, in this case, there was good reason to approach me. The producer had listened to my version of Dante's *Inferno*, another one-off adaptation of a classic, and was excited to start work. I assumed that he was willing to embrace the sort of risks that I'd taken in that production. I mean, to be clear, there was a turnstile at the Gate of Hell. It was not a literal setting of Dante's poem! But this version of the Book of Revelation was to be a dramatic and faithful transcription of the book. Any description in the original had to be faithfully reproduced. I remember on one occasion the producer saying that although he liked the sound of the Angel, it didn't seem to be coming down, and the book particularly mentions that. He was really into 'literal', whereas I was, and am, into 'figurative'[27]. We didn't fall out over these things, but I often had to limit my ideas in favour of safer and less exciting options.

There was one risk that the producer did take, though, and unwittingly. It was with the voice of God. As you can imagine, God featured quite heavily in the Book of Revelation. In fact, it wouldn't have been the same without Him. We were working through the different recording sessions over several weeks, and I could see the God session approaching, but hadn't recognised the actor that had been chosen. On the day in question, I took my place in the control room with the recording engineer, whilst the producer showed the actor into the studio. It wasn't till he sat down that I realised who it was. The Brigadier from **Doctor Who**, Nicholas Courtney. The producer had no idea who he had hired, and that put me in a rather tough position. Obviously, we had to go ahead, but I already knew it would be a problem. We would all like to think of God as an old English gentleman, but somehow picturing the Brigadier (which you did

---

[27] AKA imaginative or even allegorical (like 'The Kingdom of Colours').

as soon as you heard him) would spoil the effect.

I phoned the producer early the next day; he greeted the news with a mixture of embarrassment and concern, and we hired another actor immediately.

Derek Jacobi was to be the voice of John, the narrator. It was clear from the start of the recording session that he had done a great deal of preparation. His phrasing, intonation and the pace he delivered the lines seemed to come out of nowhere, with little prompting from the producer. Similarly, Judi Dench's introduction to the piece added such sophistication to the project that we couldn't wait to assemble it.

I was now in the circular studio with a fair degree of automation, so memorising presets and mixing became considerably easier. But we mustn't forget that there was also a digital revolution going on, and *Revelation* was created in the middle of it.

I can only blame myself for agreeing to use a DAR Soundstation on the project. I have a weakness for new gear, and one with a rosy red plasma screen was too much to resist. The suppliers were over the moon that it would be road tested on a high profile programme, and provided the machine at the drop of a hat.

It was impressive to look at, and on the face of it offered a very good digital replacement for the multitrack tape machine that had been such an invaluable resource for many years. Perhaps that was part of the problem, because in many ways it behaved more like a digital version of an analogue multitrack than a digital recorder.

Its lack of finesse was clear as soon as you turned it on. The output was not muted during startup, and gave out a deafening electronic fireworks display as the thing stabilised[28]. In the meantime, as Ray White's website testifies, the engineers were suffering a baptism of digital fire. They needed a clock to lock different equipment together so that data could flow. But this piece of early digital gear defaulted to its own clock, resulting in fizzing mayhem. The DAR Soundstation was already an unwelcome guest before I'd recorded a single thing.

We'd started using the tiny Mac Plus computers in 1985, and were now used to them. It was commonplace to be able to copy a chunk of data and insert it elsewhere.

Say you had a recording of...

Mary had a lamb
Its fleece was white as snow

and you wanted to insert the word 'little' before 'lamb'? You could simply grab 'little' and drop it in front of 'lamb'. Sensing what had happened, the rest of the text would shift later to accommodate the extra word. But if you had tried that on the DAR, it would have resulted in...

Mary had a little
Its fleece was white as snow.

It erased the audio at the insert point to fit in the new word. The only way to achieve what you wanted was to shift the rest of the text to the right (later), just enough to allow for the new word to fit into the gap. All right with a short nursery rhyme, but not great if there was 40 minutes of programme across all eight tracks to move. Of course, it was something you could never have done on an analogue multitrack either, which I suppose supports my contention that this was just a digital version of an analogue machine.

---

[28] I used a recording of the startup noises in a production as a sound effect, so it was at least worth something.

It was not long before the ease of Mac and Windows recording platforms overtook hardware such as the DAR, which was almost out of date before you took it out of the box. It made a long project even harder, but eventually a mixed programme emerged.

Its broadcast was met with very favourable reviews, and the production was entered into a religious broadcasting competition. The producer and I had high hopes of its success, but it came second. The first place was taken by a spontaneous and live local radio series, one that took about as long to produce as it did to broadcast, which was especially galling. Perhaps if more risks had been taken, and the listener surprised at every turn, *Revelation* might have taken home the trophy.

Brian Hodgson was the BBC representative on the Ars Acustica group of the EBU[29] at the time. The group was holding an audio symposium in Italy that year; a chance for European broadcasters and other performers to play examples of their work in an idyllic corner of southeast Italy called Matera. Brian suggested I accompanied him to play *Revelation*. Needless to say, I was happy to accept the invitation!

Matera is divided in two, there's a new town on the hill, and below it in a valley, the original settlement called the 'Sassi di Matera'. In 1950 the Italian authorities had declared it a health hazard, and rather than try to renovate it, moved its residents, sometimes by force, into the new town, leaving their previous homes deserted. These stone-built dwellings go back centuries, etched into the chalk rock laid out across the sides of the valley. A vast area of empty alleys and reverberant spaces.

Revelation sounded great echoing around the rocks and went down well. For me though, it was upstaged by some quite breathtaking live performances that really kindled my enthusiasm for site-specific music[30].

---

[29] Ars Acustica is a radio and sound art forum for the promotion and production of audio works within the European Broadcasting Union (EBU).
[30] Music specially devised for a given location.

My introduction to it was a simple experience, one which was such a straightforward idea, it seemed a natural event. The audience crowded into a large cave mouth amongst the empty stone houses of the Sassi, lit by pitch torches. The beginning of the performance was not signalled, but instead just invaded your consciousness. We became aware of a rippling miasma of sounds, very quiet at first, but then over many minutes coalescing into recognisable pitches and phrases. The audience's chatter had subsided with the realisation that something strange was happening. The pitches were now clearer, and the texture of the sound as well, which had a reedy quality. A series of runs and arpeggios, interspersed with lyrical motifs that were carried around the stone walls. After many minutes, we could see a movement deep in the cave in front of us, a figure holding a gold object, as yet unrecognisable. It was only when the player passed through the light from one of the torches we realised that it was a man playing a soprano saxophone. The source of the sound had been just that, but reflected so many times by the cave walls it became something fascinating and mysterious. The simplest idea, and the most magical result.

This was to be just a taster of what was to come. Another performance by a group of players[31] took place at dawn the next day. Brian and I made our way to a bridge overlooking the ravine which housed the ancient town. There were surprisingly few of us, so our view of the performance was uninterrupted. Two keyboards stood on a makeshift stage, perched amongst the roofs of the stone houses, and loudspeakers were scattered amongst the ruins to either side. The orange sun was coming up behind us, a light that became ever brighter and clearer during the performance. I have to admit that I'm not easily impressed at these events, so when the players behind each keyboard improvised some average FM sounds, I wondered whether getting up that early had been worth it.

What none of us realised was that they were not the only performers.

---

[31] Despite a lot of research I have not tracked down their name, but I remember it translating as something like 'The Ruins of Rome'

Hidden amongst the stones of the old town and apparently looking out across them to us, was another performer. His speech was not static, but came from different places in the vast stone set. He spoke Italian, but with a clarity and beauty in its delivery that just took your breath away. "È una bella mattina." It is a beautiful morning, he said, and we were all under his spell.

At first he described the surroundings, but always made them, and us, part of the moment. At one point in his commentary, he referred to us on the bridge, what we were wearing, the wind blowing our jackets, the light rising behind us and illuminating the scene. And all the time, the players on stage responded to his words and improvised a sound world that became part of the spectacle. Time really did stand still, and when it was over, the sparse audience seemed so part of the moment that they were reluctant to clap and break the mood. We never saw the performers again during our stay, and I often wonder whether they realised what a dramatic event it had been. Seeing so few of us on the bridge, they probably viewed the performance as a failure, but little did they know that each of that small group took away such a large share of what had happened.

As is often the case, the longer you're away, the more there is to do when you return. A rather highbrow show was awaiting me, produced by a celebrated producer of classical music.

Humphrey Burton always seemed to be on his way to somewhere else. He had so many engagements in a day, his personal assistant must have been a choreographer. But the time he spent with you was one hundred percent yours.

We were due to meet at 11am, and planning was essential; a long time would elapse before our stars would align again.

He was accompanied by Pat Gavin, a graphics illustrator who even then had a fearsome reputation[32]. I was honoured to be part of such a high-powered team.

Cardiff Singer of the World was a strictly classical programme, so I was not surprised to have the music proscribed from the start. Humphrey had chosen a piece of music that he wanted me to cover, the aria 'Voi che sapete' from Mozart's *The Marriage of Figaro*. We would need an opera singer to provide the top line. Pat Gavin had already made some headway with the visuals and tried the idea out on us. He suggested a travelling musical stave across the screen that featured the notes of the aria. But the black dot on every note would be replaced by a pair of red lips. When we recorded the singer, she should just sing 'Dum dee Dum's[33] not the words of the aria. Pat would then get the red lips to open and close in sync.

"Just to show you what I mean," he said. *"I put my face down on a photocopier this morning and took a picture of my lips."* His industry had not yet caught up with the world of CGI, so a lot of improvisation was necessary. He showed us his rough sketch, with these smudgy puckered lips laid out on a musical stave.

I was expecting Humphrey Burton to dismiss the idea, but to my surprise he thought it was wonderful.

"We might have some trouble getting a mezzo soprano to sing 'Dum dee Dums but leave that to me."

I suggested that we recorded the singer as soon as possible, a cappella with no accompaniment, and that I would work around her performance and arrange the instrumental backing. Classical players and singers at that time, would sometimes refuse to perform to anything in headphones[34],

---

[32] His graphics for the original opening to **Poirot** remain a stand out piece of work to this day.
[33] I'd worked on **Doctor Who**. 'Dum dee Dums' were right up my street.
[34] Less so these days.

and would run a mile from a click track[35]. This way, the performer would be in control, and Pat Gavin and myself would follow her lead.

The meeting adjourned, and Humphrey set off to persuade a singer to record the aria for us. About a week later, he rang me to say he had found a mezzo soprano willing to do it, but only if we never divulged her identity. She was an internationally famous opera singer, but in accordance with her wishes, I'll not mention her name here either.

The recording session was at 10.30am in the BBC Lyme Grove Studios, about ten days later, but the engineer and I had set up long before then. No one else appeared. Eventually, about three quarters of an hour after we were due to start, we could see Humphrey through the glass, showing our performer into the studio with great reverence. Having ushered her into position in front of the microphone, he made his way into the control room.

She had removed what looked like a mink cape and hung it over a chair. On the green light[36] she performed the aria but singing the words instead of the 'Dum dee Dum's. Humphrey went in to see her. She clearly found the idea of 'Dum-dee-Dumming' utterly ridiculous but, on Humphrey's insistence, sang a few phrases to see our reaction. It sounded ideal, and we decided to go for a take.

The whole session was over in about half an hour. At which point, the mezzo soprano picked up her cape. "My car has been waiting outside. So if there's nothing more I can do?"

It had gone well, and so did the arrangement of the music. I used samples of wine glass rims stroked with a rubber glove dipped in Fairy

---

[35] A strict metronome beat played through headphones.
[36] The green lights on stands were used as signals from the control room to the performers. Rumour has it that a famous stage actress, inexperienced in radio, whose voice was inaudible in the control room, was found performing to the green light instead of the microphone!

Liquid. Not my idea, I'm afraid, but one which harked back to the very beginning of the Radiophonic Workshop. The French performers Les Structures Sonores had fascinated Desmond Briscoe at the time of setting up the department. In fact, their studio was called an 'atelier' or workshop which might well have inspired the name of our department. The most memorable of their televised performances was on an invented instrument called the 'Crystal', a structure made out of glass tubes. I was using wine glasses, but the sound was very similar. I made individual samples of each glass and then played them on a keyboard.

A published piano arrangement of the Mozart aria served as a starting point, and as I added the glass sounds to the sound of the mezzo soprano, there came a time when the two sounds merged to make a third, and from that moment on, the piece fell into place.

There was an outcry over the Dum-dee-Dum's and the crotchety lips. I can't imagine why; it was in the 'best possible taste'.

Humphrey must have been satisfied, because he came back the following year. This time though, it was an instrumental.

Despite these occasional successes, I think we were all aware that our popularity with directors was waning. It's a matter of some debate, but I think that the music on offer from outside composers was ever more enticing. Even though our services were not charged to the programmes, directors were happy to use some of their budget to look outside the BBC for their music. Clearly that trend was to accelerate over the next ten years.

In the seventies, experiment had been all. It had been expected of us, and we were only too excited to push the boundaries for whoever walked through the door. We had no business model, because it was not a business—no money changed hands, we featured in programme budgets, but way below the total and well out of sight.

During the eighties, thanks to technical advances, we could handle bigger projects and produce music alongside composers employed outside the BBC. We were happy to keep pace, but still had the time to experiment, just as the department had done from the beginning. It was that luxury of time that had allowed Delia Derbyshire to create the unimaginable **Doctor Who**, and, with Dick Mills, to crawl on hands and knees down the long corridor looking for mistakes in the editing. It was time that allowed me to spend days with a Vocoder trying to get the choral sound for 'The Greenwich Chorus'. In short, what we offered throughout the sixties, seventies and eighties, was that image of the Radiophonic Workshop that had fascinated so many listeners and viewers. The long hours of experimenting in search of something new.

Thanks to our own budget and some forward thinking investment, we could now match the music industry outside; proud to respond to anything that was asked of us. But directors' demands were changing and the real test of our viability as a department was yet to come.

The Ominous Nineties

The Radiophonic Workshop entered its final decade. We'd started out in 1958 as that strange place up at Maida Vale producing material that could not have been made anywhere else in the BBC. Drip feeding our curious unearthly sounds into mainstream media, whetting people's appetites for the unknown.

Now, in the early nineties, we were still trying to remain loyal to our founding principles, but were less able to deliver originality. We still created sounds with Pepsi straws and iron bars, paper tears and blocks of ice, but somehow it was our need to experiment that would make us do it, not any expectation from the directors. The new gear on the High Street had made professional results quicker to achieve, and originality had dropped down the list of priorities. Material that sounded contemporary and fashionable was more in demand.

We were a service department supplying BBC programme content, so we had to create what was needed, but the number of commissions was reducing.

It would be a long, slow decline.

In 1991, in an attempt to reflect the changing times, the BBC underwent a procedure that would have not seemed out of place in **The Body in Question**. The comforting arms of Auntie BBC no longer protected its staff from the cruel world outside, but were opened to welcome it in. In came the marketplace, the competition, and the bottom line. You weren't playing for Team BBC, but for your own department, pitted against every other department.

In this new environment, the smaller entities were doomed to fail and Producer Choice, for that's what it was called, would hasten the end of the Radiophonic Workshop.

Ironically, it didn't diminish our appeal to the public, but was more of an erosion of interest from our employers. They were frequently engaged in consultations as to what this brave new world meant for the people on the shop floor, and how middle management could sell it. Our own head, Brian Hodgson, had a frustrating time trying to appease his line managers whilst encouraging us to carry on as before.

That was hard to do. The BBC Maida Vale building had always shielded us from the cut and thrust of Television Centre and Broadcasting House. Producers and directors would welcome the opportunity to come over and see us. They sensed a kind of haven for the arts; the symphony studio in the belly of the building, and along its upper rim, a series of rooms where audio experiments took place. These small makeshift cells would bring forth many wonderful baubles that they could take back to their programmes and sprinkle like fairy dust. But now we had a different identity. It's as if we were working with all the windows open, and all the magic had been blown away.

We'd seen ourselves as equal to outside composers, but had overlooked one glaring inequality. They charged for their services, we did not.

Producer Choice put a stop to that, and us 'teenagers' on the top corridor started paying rent. Our services were no longer below the line.

That barometer of morale, the Maida Vale Canteen, was now the scene of constant discussions about impending cuts. Gone were the fun lunches and endless jokes. Even the maggot in the emulsion must have lost his smile. With no relief from our work, and this steady stream of discontent, time passed slowly.

The BBC needed to justify time spent in finished broadcast minutes, which made challenging projects less viable. If we'd made our name through innovation and experiment, then we had to sustain it through a relentless drive for value.

Producer Choice had made everybody's job harder. For their part, the directors had to account for every jot and tittle, and were losing their sense of humour. Their requests were less adventurous, their thoughts drawn to the bottom line.

In the first seven years of the eighties we worked on one thousand one hundred and thirty-two projects, in the first seven years of the nineties only six hundred and sixty-eight. That number counts for even less when you look into the work itself; many minor jobs for the BBC regions and for BBC Schools.

Of course, there are always exceptions and several high profile jobs did manage to break through. For their directors, the experience was the same as anything in the eighties.

There's an old candle on my bookshelf at home; a present from the **The Strange Landscape** production office. It was a five-part series about the middle ages, and each of the programmes is named on the side of the candle. It remains unused. A reminder that there were some flashes of light in the approaching gloom.

There was much discussion about the proposed title music for this BBC2 series. There were those in the production team who wanted something more contemporary, but I was keen for it to have a strong medieval flavour. I had used a counter tenor in one section of the music for *Revelation* and was keen to use the voice again.

The counter tenor sounds different to our ears. Although sung by a man, it has a very pure flutey tone in a high register. As before[37], the voice was going to be recorded first.

I'd set up the microphone in the acoustic area alongside my studio in good time, but it was now getting late, and was already time for the session to start. I looked up at the clock again.

Perhaps my soloist was having trouble getting past reception security.

I walked down the corridor towards the front door. As I arrived a great roar echoed down the street outside, and an immaculate vintage Harley Davidson motorbike pulled up outside. The rider, in full leathers, pulled off his helmet, and marched inside.

My performer had arrived.

---

[37] For *Cardiff Singer of the World*.

Moments later, he stood in front of the mic and glanced at the score. The motorcycle helmet was on a chair beside him, and he still wore his heavy leather kit. With no further discussion, he sang through the piece with the voice of a choirboy.

An incongruous sight.

It took about a quarter of an hour to record a perfect take, at which point he thanked me for the session, jumped on his Harley Davidson and roared up Delaware Road to his next appointment.

The Power House

Berlin

It's 16th August, 2017. We are playing in the Atonal Festival in Berlin tonight

For many years, I had a small piece of the Berlin Wall in my bedroom.

I'd been on a trip with a few of my school friends to West Berlin, and I had taken it as we'd walked alongside the wall in sight of the East German guards in their watchtowers. I didn't feel that brave; it was a very small piece.

I have a particular affection for Germany, having spent many weeks every year during my teens, with a family in Pforzheim near the Black Forest. As we travelled around, I remember seeing small signs reading 'Niemals Getrennt' alongside many of the roads. 'Never Divided'. It seemed a forlorn hope in the sixties. Little did they know that almost thirty years later it would become a reality.

We are playing in one of East Berlin's former electricity power stations. It feels uncanny and also a little sad. For so many years, this part of the city was only seen from a distance, and we could only imagine what it was like to live in a militarised zone. Since the wall has come down, and Germany has re-united, the city of Berlin has become one, but still seems to have a split personality. Today, it's showing its adventurous side. The Atonal festival, staged in this gigantic venue, has a unique atmosphere.

We are on the main stage in the vast turbine hall. The acoustic's hard to describe. The echo's long, with a rich tone where even the shortest stab of a sound becomes a rich full-bodied declaration.

It's the sort of acoustic that makes you doubt your own playlist, and write something specifically for the venue. As it happens, that's roughly what we are forced to do, because a short way into our set, the main computer fails. Luckily we've just started the opening to an abridged version of 'Picasso'[38], which starts with two minutes of improvisation. Without the backing tracks coming off Mark's system, we naturally drift into a ten minute spontaneous jam that proves very popular with the audience. Our sound's moving around this great hall in long reverberant waves, and we're enjoying ourselves.

None of these concerts could happen at all without technical support, and the sudden crisis has brought Bob Earland across the stage to see what's happening to Mark's computer. Bob's no ordinary technician, being our second drummer[39] and also an electronic music composer in his own right. It looks like a simple reboot is called for, and after pouring over Mark's computer for a while, smiles break out, and the backing to 'Picasso' is added seamlessly to our electronic jazz.

There had been a discussion about whether we should play an excerpt from *Hitchhikers Guide to the Galaxy*. We assumed that its popularity in Germany might not be large enough to guarantee its success. We couldn't

---
[38] No doubt you remember the lift!
[39] There are a few numbers that require double percussion. One of them, 'Tattoo', is based on a jam session by Bob and Kieron after our soundcheck at Hamburg, Germany.

have been more wrong. The crowd of predominantly young people are so enthusiastic to hear it played on their home soil that it's one of the hits of the night. Thanks to the internet and social media, this young audience has formed a new relationship with music that was written for their parents and grandparents, when this building was generating electricity for East Berlin.

After the concert, as the final flight cases are being loaded into the van, we're invited to see the power station's control room. It's a long trek over to the far south-western corner of the building, where we take the lift up to the first floor. The corridors are dull and dusty, and the crumbling concrete crunches under our feet.

We're shown into a long rectangular room with a high ceiling, lined on all sides with control desks. The Berlin Wall came down in 1989, but these were built a lot earlier. All the surfaces of the panels are a dull grey green. Black control knobs, large and round, interspersed with gauges and meters. It reminds me of BBC studios from the sixties. Above each of them on the wall behind are hand-written notes on scraps of white paper. They list the streets affected by each of the controls; 'Sonntagstrasse', 'Kopernikusstrasse', and the most famous of them all 'Unter den Linden' (Under the Limes). There's a makeshift feeling about this room. As if the engineers have only just left, on the day the wall fell and Germany was one again.

Coming to an End

It was inevitable that the enthusiasm the Workshop had created in the public, musicians and manufacturers, would become big business. We'd ridden the waves of voltage-controlled synthesisers, FM synthesis, MIDI and digital recording. Now, with the advent of personal computers and home audio recording, our days as a specialist centre were numbered.

Anyone could buy equipment on the High Street as capable as anything we were using, and the costs of setting up a studio had plummeted. The BBC, with its new system of marketing, hired composers working out of their bedrooms, at the same time as charging the Workshop for every room it used. It was a perfect storm. Producer Choice together with the popularisation of audio on the High Street created such an unlevel playing field, it would be impossible to continue.

Despite this, there were occasional signs of hope.

It turned out that Producer Choice was not all bad. It would eventually force the Workshop to close, but meanwhile offered some unexpected bonuses. For the department's remaining years, we could work for other broadcasters. The doors had been opened to the outside world, and we were allowed to advertise our wares beyond the confines of the BBC, to anyone who was willing to pay. This resulted in me spending a lot of what remained of the nineties on work for Channel 4, whilst still employed by the BBC.

In 1994, the director of one of the most ambitious and creative documentary makers of that period had seen something that I'd done for the BBC and had asked the Radiophonic Workshop whether I was available. This was the start of a relationship with Windfall Films, which lasted until years after I'd left the BBC.

Channel 4 had commissioned them to produce a series called **The Real Jurassic Park** and, as with all of Windfall Films' output, it revolved around a fascinating idea. Would it be possible to recreate the Jurassic world of dinosaurs today, using DNA discovered in fossils and amber? A documentary differs from a drama in that there's no script, no warning of the material that will be featured, only an outline of the subject of each section of the film, and the experts that will be interviewed to explain it. A series of featured sequences are pre-planned, but their exact nature and how they will fit into the overall scheme is still open for debate. As a result, a vast amount of material lands in the edit suite on day one of post production. A daunting challenge for any team, but instead of reaching for tried and tested solutions, Windfall Films kept a very open brief. So much so, that the composer was invited in on the discussions and decisions far earlier than I'd experienced in the BBC. It was fascinating to see this whole product emerging from all the ingredients at once. A holistic approach, and although such things were not even invented, it bore an uncanny resemblance to 3D Printing[40].

We'd spent all these years content in our bubble, always wary of the outside world, only to have that bubble burst. To our surprise, we discovered we were valued more by the outside world than by the BBC. Not enough to make it a viable department under Producer Choice, but enough to rebuild the confidence that had been sapped by our own employers.

Working for commercial television was a novel experience. In the edit suite, they kept on mentioning 'bumpers'. Two or three second shots that buffered the programme either side of commercial breaks. Each of these needed a short musical sting, something that no other Workshop composer had done before. A trivial point, but it highlighted something that had previously surprised other composers. As I have already mentioned, our colleagues outside the BBC were envious of our constant stream of commissions, but were taken aback when they realised that we could not work for any other broadcaster. They, on the other hand, could work for whoever they liked[41], but then we had all the benefits of being employed by the BBC. A reasonable trade off. So, our sudden ability to work outside did come as a surprise.

The Real Jurassic Park was the first of many films I scored for Windfall Films. Series such as **The Tourist Trap** and **The Machine that Changed the World**, and my best experience of the entire decade, **Reality on the Rocks**.

---

[40] The construction of a 3D object from a pool of resources.
[41] They would have to win the job first, of course.

This was a clever idea. The challenge was to get a comic actor to understand quantum physics over the course of the series.

He started in Programme One trying to read Stephen Hawking's *A Brief History of Time*, and ended up in the last programme meeting Hawking himself. Through the use of state-of-the-art graphics and live action overlay, the comedian would be reduced to the size of a particle and walk around the quantum world, making observations as he went.

The actor they chose for this daunting journey was Ken Campbell. I can safely say that there never was, and never will be, another person like Ken Campbell. His stage shows, one of which is featured in the series, revolve around his bizarre anecdotes and strange takes on the world. A true original, who would embarrass you one moment, and make you gasp at his unexpected sense of the absurd the next. A natural for the world of Quantum Physics.

The series required me to provide themes, incidental music and manipulated sound. In short, this was true Radiophonic fare.

The following are eleven of the eighty three pieces of music across the whole series.

25	Einstein's Brain	29/7/94	Reality on the Rocks
1	Opening Sequence	27/7/94	Reality on the Rocks
2	Book 1	27/7/94	Reality on the Rocks
3	Across Bridge	27/7/94	Reality on the Rocks
18	Opening Prog 3 (1st Mix)	14/7/94	Reality on the Rocks
19	The Monk	25/7/94	Reality on the Rocks
20	P1 End Sequence with Shout	25/7/94	Reality on the Rocks

21	P1 End Sequence no Shout	25/7/94	Reality on the Rocks
22	Spectrum v2 (+piano notes)	25/7/94	Reality on the Rocks
23	Spectrum v2 (no notes)	25/7/94	Reality on the Rocks
24	Closing Music	27/7/94	Reality on the Rocks

It's both sad and telling that I had to work for Channel 4 to compose this sort of material again for a mainstream audience.

The director needed a unifying theme, which reminded us of the cosmic scale of the subject, but a light-hearted approach had to feature as well. Quite an ask. I delivered four different versions of the theme before anything worked. Jazz seemed appropriate for Campbell's clowning around, but in no way cosmic. Adding cosmic to jazz sounded like a mistake. All out cosmic was far too dramatic.

Sorting through a vast library of sounds, I came across a very obscure sample. It was of a choir singing the phonetic sounds 'Daa' & 'Doo'.

We were using a sequence from the first programme to test the new theme, where Ken Campbell was lying on a sofa, holding the book open at arm's length. The commentary tells us that although everyone claims to have read Stephen Hawking's book *A Brief History of Time*, most people can't get beyond the first couple of chapters.

I played a few long slow chords over the scene using the Daa Dee Choir sound.

It felt right, and I wrote and recorded the whole theme in the next hour. A great deal had fallen into place. The cosmic was being served by the quasi-religious sound, the humour by the Dum dee Dum.

In the last episode of the series, Campbell met Stephen Hawking in

Cambridge University. There were shots of him walking past King's College Chapel. Our awe at the scale of the cosmically large and the bafflingly small has a religious connection, and so the music seemed to fill in all the missing pieces of the jigsaw.

Felicitous moments were like gold, and rooting them out was in our DNA[42].

Despite these commissions from outside, the departmental overheads were getting too much to bear. We shed two rooms to save money. One of them, a gloomy space used for an overflow library, remained unused long after.

There's a science fiction novel in which somebody has been tampering with time, gradually causing the present to disappear. In one scene, in a Jazz Club, not only do the chairs and tables fade away but also parts of the keyboard on the piano. In the end, the pianist only has a few notes around middle C that he can play. The book's called *The Stainless Steel Rat Saves the World*[43], and in 1998 the Workshop could have done with his help. Bits of our world were falling away on a monthly basis. I was the penultimate[44] composer to leave, and had the unwelcome task of organising the leaving party for a few of the others. One every three months or so. I arranged so many framed portraits and signatures that I became well known down at the framing shop.

It seemed such a pity. We'd had our day, but that wasn't being recognised, instead we had to endure a very gradual removal of our life support, whilst appearing to still exist. It was a twist worthy of **Doctor Who**, but then even that show, which had ignited such interest in the Workshop,

---

[42] 'Felicitious' is a word used by Benny Green, the jazz saxophonist, when he reviewed my album *Through a Glass Darkly*. Very apt, and something I would never have thought of myself.
[43] Part of the **Stainless Steel Rat** series by American author, Harry Harrison.
[44] Elizabeth Parker was the one who finally put the lights out.

had also been abandoned[45]. The BBC was closing the department by a thousand cuts, but I'd have been happy to have a party. A celebration of everything that we'd achieved. I think we would have all been happy with that.

There was a feeling of disintegration, and we feared for our archive. Would all our tapes go the way of **Hancock's Half Hour?** So Paddy Kingsland, Brian Hodgson and I asked Mark Ayres whether he could start cataloguing the tapes in 1996, and by 1998, the basic catalogue[46] had been completed.

Just in time, because that was to be our last year.

The great British public had spent all those years behind the sofa, but now there was no reason for them to stay. The Radiophonic Workshop had closed.

All of us who had been in the Workshop over the last months were too shell-shocked to realise what was to happen next. Two large skips arrived outside BBC Maida Vale, and all the tapes from our library were removed to the main BBC archive in a pantechnicon. It was April 1st, the 40th anniversary of the Workshop's opening.

The Old Dog

So, that was that. The only department to be regularly mentioned in the closing credits of BBC programmes was no more. It had been a slow fadeout, which meant that its disappearance was expected, but the workshop was missed. To our surprise, the enthusiasm for **Doctor Who** continued in other ways, and we were still asked to make appearances at signings and events almost as often as in the old days.

[45] **Doctor Who** had been pulled from the schedules in 1989 by a BBC management who had tired of its waning popularity. Clearly they thought better of it in 2005!
[46] Mark and Brian continued their cataloguing off site and finally created the database that we still use today.

In 2002, Rory Hamilton and Jon Rogers, students at The Royal College of Art, asked Mark Ayres whether the ex-members of the department would like to produce some scores to accompany a visual event set in a remote quarry in Oxfordshire. The venue was not as random as it might seem. Firstly it was intended to celebrate the many scenes in **Doctor Who** adventures that were shot in quarries[47], and secondly Jon's father owned it. This unusual project, called 'Generic SciFi Quarry', rather appealed to us, and would culminate in Paddy Kingsland, Mark Ayres, and myself producing individual scores for specific parts of the evening. We had two of the strongest projectors available at the time, showing images across the whole wall of the quarry. A sound engineer more used to arena rock concerts was hired, and set up a massive surround sound system, including an extra speaker on the top rim of the quarry above the projected image.

The concert opened with a piece by Mark, featuring the long approach of a meteor from behind the audience. It whistled over their heads into the front speakers as the wall of the quarry broke up. We achieved this visual effect[48] by photographing the quarry wall and projecting the image back onto it, which then distorted as the meteor struck.

We still play an edited version of that track[49] live at our concerts.

Although this event did bring some of us back together on a project, it would be wrong to call this a full-scale reunion. It would take another seven years to achieve that.

Blundering On

Dick Mills, Paddy Kingsland, Roger Limb, Mark Ayres and I had one thing in common. We were all solitary, applied-music composers who

---

[47] Often in Wales.
[48] The brainchild of Mark Ayres.
[49] Now called 'Vortex'.

had never occupied the same room simultaneously, and who suddenly found ourselves playing a concert at the Roundhouse. It felt like learning to drive all over again.

In 2009, the venue was putting together a series of concerts under the banner 'Short Circuit', and offered us a reasonable amount of money to organise our appearance from start to finish. Unusually, there was to be no interference, so we'd only have ourselves to blame. For me, the evening didn't go as I'd hoped, but for our audience it was a night to remember. It was as if they were staring into the mysterious depths of the Radiophonic Workshop, live in front of their eyes, and their reaction was wonderful.

After the concert quite a few commentators referred to us as 'The band that never was', and in a way they'd got it about right.

The slow process of putting it together had started a few months before. The first time we gathered to try a few things out in Paddy Kingsland's studio in Hammersmith, there was a great deal of apprehension; and no wonder.

From the beginning, we'd all occupied our own space, working on our own assigned work. Only rarely did we involve anyone else from the department. This had led to a kind of tension between the composers. We had no need to play one another's music, it would have seemed ridiculous. Now, we were having to split our music into parts for the others to play, as if they were musicians at a session.

There were to be many things along the way that would come as a surprise. Things that most people would have assumed we'd done countless years before. At one point, I remember Paddy and I sitting in an adjoining room with two guitars working out the chords to the **Doctor Who** theme. There was a massive amount of catching up to do before we stood a chance of mounting this concert.

My enthusiasm for writing new material took over again, and I became engrossed in a piece called 'Dancing in the Waves'. The opportunity to create a custom-made video for it also preoccupied me. It was easy to see later that this had taken far too much time. I'd no recent experience in preparing for a live show and had underestimated how much rehearsal was necessary. I was used to learning something for as long as it took to record it and forgetting it immediately afterwards. This required a whole different mindset.

So when it came to the concert, I was able to 'walk through' all the music but totally unable to deliver a decent performance. The most crippling thing for me was the quality of sound in my earphones. The responsibility for foldback had been handed over to the Roundhouse to sort out. All of us had some problem with it but I seemed to have a major one. Although I could hear the rest of the band OK, whenever I played anything, the sound I was making was so loud it drowned out the others. It was like playing in a different house, and made the whole experience very disappointing for me. I came away, determined to do better.

During the concert Paddy Kingsland explained to the crowd, to their absolute delight, that although the Workshop had been closed in 1998, we, being British, intended to 'blunder on anyway'.

And blunder on is exactly what we have done ever since.

On the Road At Last

After the concert, many people wanted to take it further, but circumstances conspired against us. Our show had impressed the manager of The Roundhouse, who was keen to manage any future engagements for us. We were all looking forward to the relationship, but running one of the busiest and most diverse venues in London leaves no time for other projects, and it came to nothing. This was despite help from Cliff Jones, who had just met Mark Ayres at a meeting at BASCA[50], and had volunteered to supply contacts at various venues where we might perform. The project appeared to have hit the buffers, but was thankfully rescued some months afterwards, when Cliff offered to take over the management of the band.

Two things had been clear from The Roundhouse concert. Firstly that the presence of vintage gear on stage was much appreciated by the audience, and secondly that despite the Workshop output only occasionally using percussion, a drummer made the event more dynamic and exciting. We've since realised that it was those two things that set us apart from a lot of synth-based bands. It requires a great deal more preparation, and is more expensive to transport, but using vintage gear gives the audience just what they need.

After a lot of preparatory negotiating with venues and festivals, we started to design our stage rig. This time we'd take control of the feed to our earphones on stage, in fact we would take control of everything!

We currently run a very tight ship. Mark acts as the technical hub, and Roger, Paddy and myself have independent work stations that handle all our individual sounds, but receive patch[51] change commands from a timeline running on Mark's computer. This timeline also runs the videos. A personal monitoring system allows each of us to mix eight stereo audio feeds to our own personal liking. These contain the sound of yourself and everyone else, including drums and any track playback that may be needed. In addition, the last two controls (15 and 16) carry cue idents and a click track. The cue idents are voiced signals to warn of upcoming junctions, and the click track, a metronome. Different items will require a different combination of these two. The number 'Wasted Plain'[52], for instance, has no click track, but has signals for major changes, followed

---

[50] The British Academy of Songwriters, Composers, and Authors.
[51] On MIDI devices, this is a setting needed to make a particular sound.
[52] 'Wasted Plain' is a new number that has a very dystopian nightmare feel, with a bed of manipulated rhythmic sound and wild live contributions from the whole band.

by a four beat pip sound counting down to the change.

Mark's technical hub passes a series of stereo audio feeds to our dedicated mix engineer, Zoe Martin, at front of house. This is where final balancing takes place and where the live mics from the drums meet the direct audio from the band, and the final sound is fed to the PA speakers.

It's an intricate setup, but it's served us very well over many years. One of the exciting things about it, is its ability to change all of our sounds in an instant, sometimes in the middle of a song, where a whole new palette is called for. In any concert there are almost a hundred patch changes shooting across the stage, keeping the recorded tracks and our live performance in sync with the video on the screens above.

Of course nothing works all the time…

Back in Portmeirion

So here at Festival No 6 in Portmeirion, we are experiencing one of those times. You may remember that one of our laptops has decided that enough is enough, and Dick Mills has been entertaining the crowd. We're rebooted now and make our way through the rest of the set. Roger Limb's 'Incubus', my 'Astronauts', and John Baker's 'New Worlds'.

The crowd's with us all the way. I suppose we shouldn't be too surprised because the launch of the Radiophonic Workshop band has not been a wild leap in the dark. Cliff Jones, our manager, commissioned a survey to see if there was enough public interest in our hitting the road. Thankfully, the research showed public enthusiasm for the idea, or as the researcher put it, "there's a lot of love out there".

As we head into the extended **Doctor Who** theme which finishes the concert, I'm just hoping that enough of it has found its way to North Wales.

I needn't have worried.

After the gig Cliff emails us all...

> What a great gig! Im still smiling 2 days later. Lots to talk about.
> Let me know if you see any reviews.
> Great word of mouth the next day on how good it had been.

The reviews duly arrived and were good. We were on the road.

And a very long road it has been:

- Festival No.6, Portmeirion, North Wales (September 2013)
- LEAF (November 2013)
- The One Show (BBC1, 20 November 2013)
- Rough Trade (25 November 2013)
- BBC 6 Music Session (16 December 2013)
- BBC 6 Music Warehouse Project, Manchester (28 February 2014)
- Cecil Sharp House (1 March 2014)
- Belfast, The Mac (26 March 2014)
- Chichester (11 April 2014)
- Liverpool (3 May 2014)
- Glastonbury (28 June 2014)
- Henley Festival (9 July 2014)
- BBC Commonwealth Games, Glasgow (25 July 2014)
- Womad Festival (27 July 2014)
- Camp Bestival (2 August 2014)
- End of the Road (31 August 2014)
- Festival No.6 (5 September 2014)
- Bestival, Isle of Wight (7 September 2014)
- Heavenly Festival, Blackheath (14 September 2014)
- Branchage Festival, Jersey (September 2014)
- Norwich (9 October 2014)
- Stockholm (31 October 2014)

- *National Film Theatre, BFI South Bank (6 December 2014)*
- *BBC 6 Music Session (2 March 2015)*
- *Queen Elizabeth Hall, South Bank (12 April 2015)*
- *Derby Film Festival (1 May 2015)*
- *Dublin (20 May 2015)*
- *Lunar Festival (7 June 2015)*
- *Sci Fi Weekender, Wales (March 2016)*
- *Stockton (11 June 2016)*
- *National Portrait Gallery (20 January 2017)*
- *Jazz Cafe (22 March 2017)*
- *BBC National Orchestra of Wales, Geek Musique (March 2017)*
- *The Science Museum, IMAX Theatre (16 June 2017)*
- *Bluedot, Jodrell Bank (with Orbital, 8 July 2017)*
- *Atonal, Berlin (16 August 2017)*
- *BBC 6 Music Session (27 September 2017)*
- *Sensoria (Sheffield, 7 October 2017)*
- *The British Library (13 October 2017)*
- *Sci Fi Weekender (24th March 2018)*
- *The Elgar Room, Royal Albert Hall (May 2018)*
- *Elbphilharmonie Hamburg (June 2018)*
- *Bluedot Festival (July 2018)*
- *Goonhilly Moon Landing Anniversary Concert (July 2019)*

For a group of composers hidden in a BBC department to suddenly find themselves on the road may seem unlikely, but with the help of Cliff Jones, and Andrew Curley, our live agent, we've peddled our wares up and down the UK, including the Commonwealth Games in Glasgow, Glastonbury, and the Queen Elizabeth Hall on London's South Bank. We've also managed to haul our long suffering gear to Dublin, Jersey, Stockholm, Berlin, Hamburg and.... the Isle of Wight. Such is the average age of this band, we need to be housed, fed and watered. There has been no sleeping in the back of the van, but decent accommodation at every turn. All of which needs some painstaking organisation and the hoovering up of most of our fees. The concerts have not made us much money, but the experience has been wonderful.

At the same time, we became involved in other projects. Strange, I know, but the Radiophonic Workshop had never scored a feature film until *Possum* in 2018. Twenty years after the Workshop had closed! In 2019, we were commissioned to write a 30 minute concert piece to celebrate the anniversary of the moon landings. 'Belonging' formed part of our set at Goonhilly, as the sun set behind one of the dishes that had received communications from the moon in 1969. We released the four album set, *Burials in Several Earths* in 2017 under our own label 'Room 13' and more are planned.

Above all, the concerts have provided me with an exciting platform for new ideas.

We play music composed over thirty years ago, alongside music that was written in the last few months. The ideas are not compromised by any narrative, or house style, and seem a lot more genuine as a result. I haven't experienced that feeling since making those five albums with John Ferdinando before joining the BBC.

Clearly, not everything is acceptable for the band or accepted by the band. Some things are studio based pieces that wouldn't transfer to the concert platform, and these are going to appear on a solo album called *Something in the Wire*[53]. A collection of tracks that will be the product of everything that's gone before; the early psychedelic folk, the applied music for the BBC, and new experimental compositions. Critics and reviewers are always keen to explain the new by referring to the old; something that used to irritate me until I could see it applying to myself!

---

[53] That is what it's called at the time of writing. Record producers have a habit of changing titles as you will realise by now.

The Royal Albert Hall

60 Years

Four Years and eight months after our first outing in Portmeirion, we are here in the Elgar Room at the Royal Albert Hall. 2018 is the 60th anniversary of the founding of the Workshop and there's a sense of celebration.

This is a venue that underlines everything rewarding about performing live. The audience stands in a space that's quite shallow, but unusually wide. The stage is not too high and allows a good contact between players and spectators.

Hundreds of people have turned out tonight. It's only natural for them to associate certain pieces with certain times. Remembering how and where they bought a record and listened to it for the first time. Playing and discussing it with friends, playing it till the grooves wore away, or until their parents begged them to stop.

So here they are at the Albert Hall, having the time of their lives. Re-living the time of their lives.

After most of our shows, we get reviews. Mostly in scifi mags (actual and online), but occasionally in the mainstream press. In all of them, there's an abiding theme: to witness something that was previously only available through your television. To spot something intriguing on air, and eventually track it down, and meet it face to face.

Here's an edited extract from a review by Alasdair Stuart on the *SciFi Bulletin* website…

Review: Radiophonic Workshop
Elgar Room, Royal Albert Hall, May 26, 2018

I don't believe in bucket lists.

But if I had a bucket list, last night I would have crossed an item off it.

Seeing the Radiophonic Workshop play in the Elgar Room at the Royal Albert Hall was deeply weird and profoundly wonderful[54]. The Workshop were pioneers of electronic music in the most literal sense of those words. Along with titans like Delia Derbyshire, these men were, and are, musicians and engineers[55] in equal measure, and the cheerful way they went about assembling an entire genre of music still echoes up and down today.

What really came across last night was the joy these people feel in doing work that has defined their lives and the lives of so many others.

There's a special kind of excitement at play here, and it's a mixture of discovery, nostalgia, and a hefty chunk of the reviewer's personal history. Some of the remarks about the early days come across as exaggerations, especially to someone like me who was there, floundering amidst the technical chaos with a deadline to meet. But it does illustrate, how after all this time there are enough enthusiastic people to fill a venue and make

---

[54] I guess one out of two isn't bad.
[55] We were not engineers, but, like any musician, were just well versed in the 'instruments' we were using. It's just that our instruments had only just been invented.

a concert worthwhile, and I know that we all feel indebted to them.
And one more thing...

You are what you can't stop doing, or so they say, and I can't stop writing music. These unavoidable gaps keep opening up and they need to be filled, so I compose. Sadly, what you can't stop doing may be unacceptable in polite society or worse still, a terrible earner. So when choices have to be made, and higher education beckons, we reluctantly go for the safe option. However, often, despite our best efforts, we just can't do what's expected of us.

It's difficult to believe now, but I left school to study law.

My teachers had made a rather pathetic attempt to advise me on my future career, but they only knew about the army, the church or the law[56]. As it happened, my father was a solicitor, so I reluctantly agreed to give the law a try. After a few years of study and practical experience, and two attempts to pass the exams, my father took me to one side and asked me what I really wanted to do. A generous gesture on his part, although he might also have been trying to save the family's reputation.

"I want to work for the BBC," I said.

This decision hadn't just come out of the blue, because for many years, I'd been interested in audio and music, and had been running my own studio in my parents' house in Hove. It was in that studio I remember being startled one day to discover that I could extemporise on the guitar. I'd previously been learning Shadows numbers rather woodenly and was surprised that I could invent stuff myself.

I am of the firm belief that every single person has talent in something, and I'm so grateful that I was able to discover mine early enough.

---

[56] You've guessed it. It was a public school. And it was 1968.

I remember I referred to this newfound gift as 'Angel Music'. Childish, I know, and it seems ridiculous now, but it was such a revelation. To make something out of nothing. A few moments before, the room was empty of ideas. Now there was something new. It just seemed incredible.

In fact, this sense of incredulity has remained to this day, and sometimes I can't believe how much I've managed to compose over the years. So much so that if, and I realise that this is another mental flight of fancy, if I was to be asked to do **Desert Island Discs**, I'd have to take a couple of my own tracks just to prove to myself that it had happened. I remember a singer appearing on that show and being ridiculed for suggesting her own performances, but I understand it. If it was me, I would be sitting on the beach of the desert island, running the sand through my fingers and muttering *"not bad for a failed solicitor from Hove"*.

But all this hasn't arrived in the normal way. I didn't study music but just 'picked it up'. This 'join the dots' approach to expertise would have been of little value if it hadn't been for the Radiophonic Workshop. That was the one place where such skills were valued, and I feel very lucky to have been at the right place at the right time, with my hotchpotch of ideas and burning desire to make them into something new.

It was that question that my father asked, *"What do you really want to do?"* that opened up a world of possibilities for me, and I'll be forever grateful for that.

So, to those parents trying to persuade their obsessively musical children to study to be a vet, a solicitor, a dentist, a rocket scientist, I would say this. If people other than close relatives voluntarily say how much they like your children's music, and if every time your offspring should be studying they are writing music and if despite their best efforts they appear to be pretty useless at anything else, just bear this in mind. You might be denying them something in which they would excel, something they would love to do, not just for a career, but for the rest of their lives.